MEET THE PRINCIPAL

My Journey Beyond the Curriculum

JANE BLOMSTRAND

AltPublish.com

Meet the Principal: My Journey Beyond the Curriculum by Jane Blomstrand

©2019 Jane Blomstrand

Print Edition ISBN: 978-1-7332459-0-6

UPDATED and retitled edition (Originally: "Beyond the ABCs: What Does a Principal Do All Day?" Dec 2018 ISBN:978-1941713938) This edition includes new chapters and updated details.

Cover 'Hands' by Megan Majestic

Layout by William Gensburger

Website: www.MeetThePrincipal.com

Alt Publishing: P.O. Box 51, Emmett, ID. 83617 | www.AltPublish.com

Ordering Information: Orders by U.S. trade bookstores and wholesalers. Please contact Ingram Book Company, ipage: https://ipage.ingramcontent.com

Printed in the United States of America

Dedicated to:

My grandchildren, Riley, Olivia, Ava and Emmet for giving me the inspiration to write this book by asking me, "What <u>DOES</u> a principal do all day?" *And for caring enough to listen to my stories.*

What Readers Said...

"This book not only allows you an insight into the daily life of a principal; the heartbeat of a school, but it offers a glimpse of what the job entails for future administrators." ~M. Dolley, Principal

"I highly recommend reading this book. Jane Blomstrand does an excellent job at explaining how difficult it is for a school to rise above its challenges. She gets the reader to try to understand the dance between teacher, student, parent and curriculum. I found myself underlining and making notes, and saying out loud, YEP! A must read even if you are not in education."
~M. Haase, Teacher

"This book is a "must read" for anyone who wants an exceptionally honest and poignant account about the incredible world school principals face each day. Jane Blomstrand's wonderful vignettes beautifully capture the complex, exciting and often unpredictable situations our school leaders must continually navigate, often on a daily basis."
~R. Zinn, Superintendent (retired)

"I've never really thought much about what school principals do all day. Now I will after reading Jane Blomstrand's book. This is an excellent book for anyone who has a child in school or works in a school. The stories are fascinating and I was sorry when the book ended."
~J. Evans, Parent

A REQUEST FROM THE AUTHOR

After you have read this book PLEASE take a moment to leave me a brief, honest review. You may do so where you purchased the book (Amazon, Barnes and Noble…) or on the book site at:

www.MeetThePrincipal.com

Thank you,

Jane Blomstrand, *Author*

Contents

THE FIFTH INNING

THE SIXTH INNING

THE SEVENTH INNING

Principals are Like Baseball Managers

I am a dedicated baseball fan. When I first became a school principal I thought about what it meant to be a good manager and coach. How did people like Tony LaRussa, Bruce Bochy and Bob Melvin do it? Each successfully managed a team of outstanding, independent baseball players and a staff of coaches, while trying at the same time to please a stadium of fans and meet the demands of the front office and owners. They had to work together and constantly make decisions based on what they thought was right to produce a winning baseball team.

As a school leader I believed I was like these managers. I was responsible for a school of 720 students and over 60 teachers and support staff, while at the same time being accountable to the district office, the school board and the parents. It was critical we all worked together and do what was right to create a winning school team.

Each day offered challenges, many unpredictable, depending on who called on the phone or walked in the office door. Every day also offered rewards, like getting a high-five from that student who last week spent time in my office. Like a baseball manager, I was required to think on my feet, react appropriately and follow through in an effective manner, putting the right people in the game.

For most of my career as a principal I worked in an ethnically diverse community. Nearly 45 percent of our students were English learners, and close to 75 percent qualified for free or reduced lunch. After I retired I was asked to work as an interim principal in a school district where less than 3 percent of the students were English learners and less than 2 percent qualified for free and reduced lunch. Even though the districts appeared very different on paper they had more in common than people might think. Just as all baseball teams have great ballplayers, good coaches and excited fans, both of the districts I worked in had excellent teaching staffs, caring parents and energetic students ready to learn.

The stories in this book are about my many experiences with students, parents and teachers attempting to create a winning educational environment.

When my grandkids started school they asked me questions like, "What do principals do all day?" So, upon retirement, I decided to start recording these stories to pass on to my family. I enrolled in a local Adult Education Creative Writing Class to develop some writing skills. At each session we were asked to bring a new piece of writing to class. That was perfect! I could write and share a story every week.

As I shared these experiences, participants in the class made comments like, "I love hearing your stories, I learn so much from them," "I had no idea principals had to do that." It made me realize that not only did my grandkids have little idea of what principals do, but also much of the general population didn't either. We've all had our own experiences in school, but most of that comes from the perspective of being a student, parent or maybe a teacher. Few have the perspective of what it is like to be the leader of a school.

My classmates started telling me, "You need to put these experiences in a book." Their comments made me think that there could be an expanded audience. Maybe other principals would like to read stories that describe encounters similar to what they had experienced. Maybe those interested in becoming school administrators would like to hear what really happens when you are a school leader; or maybe some people would just be interested in reading about what goes on in the life of a principal.

So here is my collection of stories. All principals have stories like these whether they work in an elementary, middle or high school. The names are fictional, except mine, but each story is true. For the sake of easy reading I intentionally use the same district name throughout the book, but similar stories happened in both districts I worked in.

You might be surprised if you knew which story came from which district, but each has, at its core, one or more relationships that were built and then hopefully impacted that school culture in a positive way. Some stories are funny, some are sad, and some may touch your heart. When you put them together, hopefully you will have experienced what happens at a school beyond the curriculum.

THE FIRST INNING

IT SHOULD HAVE BEEN THE FIRST DAY OF SCHOOL!

The Asbestos Challenge

*I*t was the day before students would arrive for the beginning of school and classroom assignments had already been posted in the windows of the lobby. I had slowly driven back to school after purchasing several items for my new office and, after getting out of my car, looked out at the expansive lawn and huge sycamore trees, admiring Baxter's serene setting. The walkway to the double door entrance was inviting with flowers some of the teachers and I had freshly planted last week. Doing that gardening project together had been a great way to become better acquainted.

What a whirlwind that last month had been getting to this point! I interviewed the end of July, left that afternoon for a two-week vacation and now school was set to begin tomorrow. I was excited to begin my first job as an elementary school principal. I looked forward to the challenge facing me with nervous excitement. Thousands of questions still raced through my mind as I walked toward the entrance. Was I prepared for this job? I had never been a vice-principal, so didn't have much experience preparing me for principalship. I was about to find out in the morning when all 720 students would arrive.

I took a deep breath and as I approached the large glass doors of the lobby I could see several people inside. I recognized Don, the Superintendent, Leann, the Assistant Superintendent of Business, Wayne, Assistant Superintendent of Human Resources, and Tim, Director of Maintenance. Standing with them were four unfamiliar men dressed in suits.

Don greeted me. "Welcome to Robinson, Jane. Your school is contaminated with asbestos and classes can't begin here tomorrow."

I stared at him. His serious expression told me he was not kidding. I felt a tightness in my chest. Everyone was staring at me. I took a deep breath to maintain my composure. This was no time for feelings to take over. My head was swimming with questions. *Did I hear him correctly? What does this mean? What do we do if we can't open school tomorrow? How do we notify parents? etc, etc, etc....*

What was probably four seconds seemed like an eternity. Don put his hand on my shoulder. "Let's go into your office where we can talk."

As the nine of us squeezed around my tiny conference table, Don introduced everyone.

"This is William Spencer and Justin Blackman from the Department of Occupational Safety and Health Administration (OSHA), and Jared Broadman and Martin Espinosa from Parmen, a local engineering firm. We've been walking through the classrooms to see what the situation is and how it can be rectified."

I was trying to process what this meant. Workers had just finished re-roofing the school. Rusty had alerted me that the force of nailing had caused asbestos particles from the ceilings to filter down into some classrooms. I knew asbestos could be an issue but they had cleaned everything up and I thought the problem had been resolved.

Don continued, "We've brought these gentlemen in to look at the ceilings and let us know if the classrooms are safe for students. Apparently they're not and they need to be fixed, so school can't begin until the ceilings are repaired."

I sat quietly and listened as the group discussed what to do with the students and teachers. Don asked if there were empty classrooms at other schools. Could the students arrive at Baxter and then be bused to different schools? Tim listed the various empty classrooms throughout the district, some at elementary schools, some at middle schools and some at the high school. "Yes, that would work," he said. "We have enough classrooms to house all students and their teachers."

You have got to be kidding, I thought. *My teachers have spent hours preparing for school starting tomorrow, all of their teaching supplies are in their classrooms, and they can't get into them because of the asbestos. You can't spread them out all over the city, with no materials and no support. What about the buses, how would they transport our students all over town?*

I fought back frustration as I tried to keep calm while expressing these concerns to the group. I felt vulnerable. All these people sitting around the table were experts in their fields with years of experience, and here I was, a brand new principal on the job for less than three weeks. After much discussion, I boldly asked a question. "Is it ever possible to delay the opening of school for a few days in an emergency like this? Could the missed days be made up at the end of, or during, the school year?"

They all looked around at each other, and finally Leann replied. "Yes, that is possible. The state allows a school district to apply for a waiver in situations like this, and instructional minutes lost can be made up during the remainder of the school year."

Whew, I thought, *at least there's an option to farming our teachers and students out all over the district.*

Discussion continued with other options being offered by the group. Finally, Don leaned his large frame over the table and onto his elbows. He paused for a few seconds looking directly at me. It felt like 10 minutes of his eyes piercing mine. Finally he responded.

"Well, Jane, this is your school. What do you propose we do?"

I looked back at him for what seemed like an eternity. It felt as if I had a mouth full of cotton balls. Thoughts percolated in my head. *I just became a principal. How am I supposed to know what to do? Is this one of those big decisions you asked my former superintendent if I could make?*

I felt like a pitcher in the bottom of the ninth inning with a 1-0 lead, a runner on third, 2 outs, a 3 ball 2 strike count facing him and a stadium full of fans standing up, yelling and clapping to see what he would do. What *would* he do? He couldn't disappoint his team and the fans; they would be counting on him to get the job done. He had to pitch!!!

So, without hesitation, I asked a question. "How long will it take to repair the ceilings?"

"About 4-5 days."

"Then," I said, "I suggest we delay the opening of school for one week and make up the instructional minutes during the remainder of the school year."

Everyone at the table looked at each other.

"That sounds like a good plan," said Don.

They all agreed with that decision as the best course of action to take. I breathed a huge sigh of relief as we ended the meeting. We wouldn't have to farm teachers and students out all over the school district, but now our work would begin, informing the teachers, students and parents plus putting a plan of action into place for the next week.

I had been put to the test and hopefully I had passed.

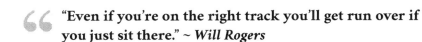

 "**Even if you're on the right track you'll get run over if you just sit there.**" ~ *Will Rogers*

What Do We Do Now?

*D*ecisions had to be made quickly because 40 teachers and 720 students were going to show up the next day, which was supposed to have been the first day of school. Now they needed to know what to do and where to go.

Don peppered me with questions.

"Jane, how do you want to handle this? When will you tell the teachers? How will you let the parents know not to bring their kids to school tomorrow?"

My head was spinning; they were all looking at me. Beads of perspiration formed on my brow and my face started to flush. *Shove that panic feeling aside,* I thought. *I have to make decisions. Where to start? Teachers first, they needed to know what was happening. Parents next, they needed to make plans for their kids.*

The teachers were currently attending professional development at another school in the district and we decided to call them back for a briefing on the situation before going home.

The best way to let parents know seemed to be for teachers to call the home of every student in their class as soon as possible. I asked Janet, the school office manager, to prepare class lists to hand out.

~~~

After the teachers arrived back at school, Don and I met with the entire staff. He explained about the asbestos. They listened quietly and then asked a few questions.

"How will our families know not to bring their kids tomorrow?" asked Paula, one of our first grade teachers.

"We are preparing class lists for each of you and are asking that each of you call the families on your class list and let them know. We have prepared a script for you to use if you need it," explained Don.

"Many of us have personal things in our classrooms," said Barry. "Are we allowed to go in quickly and get them?"

"Yes, but just this once until we have the abatement completed," he continued. "Also, Jane and I agreed that in the morning you all would be out in front of the school to greet any parents who didn't get the message and any students who walked to school. "

Whew! First steps complete. I sat down and breathed a sigh of relief. Don and Leann were still in my office but I wished I had been alone at this point. I just wanted some time to let it all sink in. I couldn't show them how unsure I was about what should happen next. I felt as if I had to appear completely confident, knowing what to do, but this wasn't one of the things they prepared new administrators for at the university. In fact, I was willing to bet even Don had never before been through this exact situation. There was no time to feel sorry for myself. Decisions still had to be made regarding what the staff would do all day long next week without students.

"Jane," Don asked. "Do you have a place where you can meet with all your teachers for the next five days? The library ceiling has to have asbestos abatement also, so you can't use it, and your faculty room would be too packed with all of you in there. "

"Does the park across the street have a meeting room? If so, can we reserve it? We could meet there each morning to make plans."

I asked Janet to contact the park and the meeting room was quickly reserved. One step down!

After having a discussion about how to make up five days of instructional time during the rest of the school year, and asking me to let them know as soon as possible what the rest of my plans for the teaching staff would be, Don and Leann left.

~~~

What were my plans for the staff? What can you do with a staff of teachers who had prepared for teaching the next day, with all of their teaching materials in the classrooms they couldn't get into? My head was swimming.

Before I had too much time to think about it Gina and Karla came into my office. They were sisters who taught second grade and kindergarten.

"Jane, we were thinking it would be nice to have coffee and pastries in the morning and we're volunteering to bring everything and get it all set up. Do you know where we'll be meeting?"

"Oh my gosh, that's so nice of you. It's about the only thing I do know right now. We have the meeting room at the park across the street for the next week; we'll all meet there first thing each morning. Having coffee and treats would be terrific; I'll take you up on that and the school will pay for it. Thanks so much for offering. It takes one thing off my mind."

"Don't even think about it for the next five days. We'll make sure to have treats and coffee each morning. You have enough to be concerned about, you don't need to be worrying about feeding everyone."

I thanked them profusely and they left. Having Gina and Karla volunteer like that might not seem like a big thing to some people, but to me, at that time, it was a huge gift. It helped lift my spirits and made me feel that we were a team. Now there was a plan in place to start off each day.

I took out a pad of paper and started jotting down ideas of what we could do for the next five days: #1. Observe teachers at other schools. I would check with the other principals to see if that was possible.#2. Plan time each day to collaborate as grade levels. #3. Brainstorming as a group about school procedures. #4. Work on projects around the school that need completion. The list began to grow as I wrote down constructive ideas for my teachers to do during the next five days.

We had eight staff members new to the school that year, including me, so as we met in the park each morning, new and experienced teachers collaborated together making good use of this perfect opportunity to engage in team-building activities. We transformed our six portable classrooms into grade level meeting rooms so each afternoon every grade level had time to meet together and plan curriculum. All teachers had the opportunity to spend a day observing teachers at other schools in the district. It was a very organic process.

What started out as a dark cloud turned out to have a silver lining. The teachers and I had time to get to know each other before students arrived. We laughed and got grungy working on the projects together. It was a unifying experience. If you asked any teacher who taught at Baxter School that year, they would tell you that it was the most unusual and satisfying start to school they had ever experienced.

 "I not only use all the brains that I have, but all that I can borrow." *~Woodrow Wilson*

THE SECOND INNING

IT'S THE PEOPLE THAT MAKE THE DIFFERENCE!

Lining Up Before School

inally, the first day of school arrived and it was an eye opener for me. The day started before classroom instruction began at 8:30 a.m. Over half of our students arrived on buses from different parts of the city, making us a "bussing school." The other students walked, were dropped off by family members, or arrived in various carpools.

The students who came in cars and those who walked were allowed to arrive 15 minutes before the first bell rang and go play in the yard where there was teacher supervision in place. First through fifth graders who were bussed usually arrived, depending on the bus schedules, before 8:15 a.m. and, assuming they arrived on time, I went out to the yard that first morning to chat with them. I got there a little before 8:15 a.m. but to my surprise I saw only a few students were there. As I was talking with students I saw Barry, a third grade teacher, coming toward me.

"Hi Barry, don't we usually have more kids out here before school starts?"

"They'll be arriving in droves any time now, but most of them come on the bus, so they line up on the side of the school after being dropped off. One of us on duty goes out to pick them up at 8:15 and bring them back here. I'm on my way right now. Want to join me?"

"I guess I hadn't been aware of that practice." Obviously this was a procedure we had overlooked discussing the previous week while we were on *Asbestos Postponement.*

We walked across the yard to the side of the school and turned left towards the front parking lot. I could smell freshly cut grass from the field on our right. To our left as we approached the front of the school there was a 2-foot high brick planter filled with dirt. Adjacent to it was a packed down gravel walkway where the bussed students waited.

I could hear the sound of student voices as we approached. Loud sounds. As we came around the corner I saw a mob of kids, at least one busload milling around, chasing each other, yelling, and some kids just talking.

I looked at Barry. "Does this go on every morning?"

That's when we saw two students on top of the brick planter getting ready to jump off.

"Hey," called Barry. "Off the planter. You guys know the wall is off limits."

Hearing Barry, the students eased their way down off the brick wall.

"Oh, hi Mr. Voght, I'm sorry. We were just getting Carlos's lunch. Marty threw it up on top of the wall."

Barry and I looked at Marty who was slipping behind Cecilia, a fairly large girl with long dark hair.

"Marty, did you throw Carlos's lunch up there?"

"Well, he was calling me names and bothering Cecilia."

This was chaos: two busloads of first through fifth graders waiting on the side of the school with no supervision. I looked at Barry.

"Was it like this last year?"

"Yep, it's like this every morning," he laughed. "Many mornings start off with a fight out here, and you'll start your day off with those kids in your office."

We looked back at Carlos and Cecilia who had calmed down.

Barry continued. "If they don't get caught, the resentment can carry over into the classroom, morning recess or lunch recess and you'll have more office visits."

"How do the teachers feel about this drop off procedure?" I asked.

"They hate it. They don't like the negative impact it has at recess and in their classrooms."

With that we blew the whistle, quieted everyone down, and walked the students out to the yard where proper supervision was waiting. I could see we needed to have some conversations with the staff about how to resolve this situation. It certainly wasn't working well the way it was.

After the bell rang I walked back to my office. Waiting for me were three third grade boys, including Marty and Carlos. The aftermath of the morning lineup had begun.

That week we held staff discussions about altering the procedure for lining up before school. We asked the maintenance department to paint lines for each grade level on the main walkway in front of the building. The next week students started lining up on the newly painted lines. It was a positive move in more ways than one. Not only did we reduce chaos and fighting but also we started a new tradition of saying the Pledge of Allegiance, and beginning our day together as a community.

 "Nothing happens unless something is moved." ~*Albert Einstein*

The Custodian

*R*usty Franklin was the sort of person who would give you a friendly greeting at the door with a slap on the back, but there were also times if you asked him to do something that wasn't to his liking you could pretty much expect a snarl. He was head custodian at Baxter and he was anything but a wallflower. Rusty was a body builder, tall, with dark hair. Much to his liking he had been allowed to wear tank top T-shirts to work. He was also very flirtatious with the female staff.

When I first met him, I noticed the extremely long fingernail he sported on his right pinkie. *That's odd*, I thought, *why would he have such a long fingernail?* I guess that was pretty naïve of me because when my friend, Nathan, came to visit he commented: "I see your buddy does cocaine."

"What?"

"Didn't you notice his fingernail?"

"Yeah I did, but I didn't know that's what it was about."

I still don't know if that was a true assessment. I never saw any evidence of it, but if it were it would explain his mood changes from very friendly one moment to petulant and angry the next.

~~~

Rusty and I had a two-week honeymoon period. He polished everything in sight and tripped over his feet trying to please me. He inquired about where I lived, did I have children, where had I worked before coming to Baxter. He chatted with me about how he grew up in Robinson, and how he graduated from Robinson High School where he had met and married his high school sweetheart. He had volumes of information about Robinson and would tell all sorts of tales about the people who lived and worked in the community. He even started wearing the district required custodian shirt.

But the honeymoon ended one 98-degree day, about a week before school was to start. The office staff had fans blowing at their desks; we were all feeling the heat and staying inside to keep cool. However, the day before we'd had some desks and chairs delivered that needed to be moved from one side of the school to the other.

Rusty and I had discussed this when the furniture was delivered, and he knew it needed to be done by the end of today. It would have been wise to complete the move in the morning when it was cooler. Unfortunately, the furniture had not yet been moved and it was after lunch when I found Rusty to remind him. He was outside hosing off the patio.

"Rusty," I called. "You know those desks and chairs that were delivered yesterday? Just a reminder, we need to have them moved to Room 28 before you leave today."

"Oh man, I can't do that today, it's too hot, it's 98 degrees outside," he grumbled. "I'll do it first thing in the morning."

"I wish we could do it tomorrow morning, but the desks and chairs need to be in that classroom *this* afternoon."

Rusty was facing the street with his back to me. My comments were met with silence. The next thing I heard was the sound of the hose being slammed against the concrete. I glared at his back. Did he actually think he could intimidate me with this little tantrum? I took a deep breath and said with confidence, "Thanks Rusty, I appreciate you getting it done before you leave today," and I walked back into the building.

I wasn't sure how things would go after that, but he did have all the furniture moved into the classroom by the end of the day. From that day forward Rusty and I worked together well. I wouldn't say it was a marriage made in Heaven, but he understood what was important to the school and me, and I learned how to work around his ego.

He Wasn't Much Help!

*T*rying to make something happen when a key person involved is unwilling to cooperate can be a huge obstacle to moving forward. A week into my job, Robin, our new first grade teacher, stopped by my office. She was tall with shoulder-length dark hair, and she had an infectious smile. I could detect a mixture of stress and excitement in her voice.

"What should I do about Brad's things that are still in my classroom?"

This was Robin's first teaching assignment. I had hired her three days before, about a week before the start of school. She had just graduated from university and was here today excited to get her classroom ready. Twenty eager little first-graders would be arriving next week and she wanted to make sure she had everything prepared for them.

Brad was the teacher who had taught in that room for the previous eight years, but was no longer teaching at the school. I had never met him but heard he was the teacher union president and had been transferred to another school against his will, to teach music. My understanding was that he had missed almost a third of the classroom instructional days last year because of union meetings, and the district felt, because he had a music background, it was better to have him teaching music than first grade.

"Let's go down to your room so I can see what he has in there," I told Robin. "I assumed he'd removed all his things, but it sounds like that's not the case."

Robin led the way and when we arrived I was surprised at what I saw. There were book shelves, packing boxes full of books, computers, a couple of file cabinets, and numerous other items stacked in a four to five foot square in the center of the room.

For a moment I just looked then I found my voice. "I can see these belong to Brad. He has his name taped all over them. I'm surprised. It almost seems as if he placed all this here to move and then forgot about it."

"That's what it seems like to me," Robin said, "but some of the other teachers told me he was really upset about being transferred and they felt he may have left his things here on purpose. I really don't know what to do. Shall I just keep working around them?"

"No," I told her. "Brad's items need to be moved out of your classroom. I'll contact him."

I returned to my office and made a phone call.

"Hi Brad, this is Jane Blomstrand, the new principal at Baxter. We just hired a first grade teacher and she'll be using your old classroom. As you can imagine she's chomping at the bit to get her room ready for students. We noticed some of your teaching materials in there. Are these things you still want? If so, can you come by and pick them up soon?"

His response completely shocked me. "The district reassigned me to another school over the summer so I've been slammed getting my new classroom ready. My contract begins in one week, the day before school starts. I'll come for my stuff that morning."

~~~

I guess I was a little naïve to think he would just pop right over. I assumed because he was union president, he would want to be as supportive as possible to a new teacher. But, I understood this was a matter of principle; he wasn't going to move anything before his contract started. I quickly had to think of a way to solve the situation; I thought maybe I could appeal to his compassion.

"Would it be possible for you to come sooner to allow Robin time to set up her classroom?"

"No, sorry," was his curt reply. "I'll be coming the first day I'm paid to return."

Well, that didn't work. But Robin still needed more time to set up her classroom, and she was looking to me for support. It was obvious Brad wasn't going to be moving anything soon. At this point there seemed to be only one solution.

"I understand your position," I told him. "Since our new teacher needs more than one day to set up for the start of school, I'll have the custodian move your things into the small hallway outside of the room. They'll be ready for you to pick up any time after today."

I could tell that decision didn't make him happy, but I had no other option. Rusty moved all Brad's possessions out into the hall and Robin was able to prepare the classroom for her students.

True to his word, Brad came for his belongings the day before school started.

 "We don't see things as they are, we see things as we are." ~*Anais Nin*

A Third Grade Teacher

*B*arry was the sort of person who would wear his Mickey Mouse hat and tie all day long and stay after school to help students or other teachers with their concerns. He was always using technology as an engaging way to enhance student learning.

I learned about his technology expertise one night when I was wrestling with how to present myself, and the staff, at Back to School Night. In addition to my being new on campus, we had seven new teachers and I was struggling to find a way to introduce who we were to the parents, and what our mission was at Baxter.

It was about five o'clock that October evening, and almost dark outside. I was in my office pondering my introduction when I heard a voice.

"Hey there, you look deep in thought."

It was Barry on his way out the door to go home.

"Oh hi Barry, what are you doing here so late?"

"I was just putting finishing touches on a PowerPoint for the kids tomorrow. We're studying 'Our Community' and I took some photos of different places throughout the city. I want them to be able to see the rich history of Robinson. What are you doing here so late?"

"I'm trying to figure out what I want to do for the introduction for Back to School Night."

"Hmmm, what are you thinking of doing?" he asked.

"Well, actually something like you just mentioned you're doing for your students tomorrow. I want to engage the parents visually, not just have me talking. I was trying to figure out how I could show photos of teachers interacting with students. Parents love to see photos of their kids."

Barry immediately tossed his backpack down and we began brain storming about what might be effective in capturing the parent's attention and getting my desired message across.

"You know, you could add some music to the background. That would put a real pop into the presentation. For example maybe a song like 'I Believe I Can Fly' as you're flashing pictures of each of the teachers with students on the screen. That could be very powerful, but beware; you'd better have mucho boxes of Kleenex on hand."

We worked for the next hour and a half tweaking the presentation specifics. We added photos of kids on the playground, students reading with teachers, small groups of students working together, and lots of other photos of teachers and students together. We made sure every teacher was represented in a photo. We were both so excited, Barry more so than I, that we didn't realize what time it was. I'm not sure if it was because of the presentation we had just prepared, or the fact that he had contributed so much to making it what I was looking for.

That's the kind of guy Barry is. He gets so wrapped up in other people's needs he forgets about his own. I finally had to kick him out of my office at about 8:30 p.m. to get him to go home to his family.

Author Footnote: Barry has now been a principal for 13 years in the same district, despite telling me never to take him out of his cave. He just has a different cave now . . . .

"Ideas are great arrows, but there has to be a bow." ~*Bill Moyers*

Hiring Gambles Pay Off

I am very grateful that I have made many good bets when hiring teachers. It's a big risk when you think of the impact they have on students. You want to make sure you have the right people in place, with the right kind of skills to do the job. Sometimes you need to rely on your instincts. Once I missed the jackpot, but most of the time we struck gold.

In one instance it was one month into the school year and our enrollment increased unexpectedly in the third grade so I had to create an additional class. Finding a quality new teacher when the school year had already started was risky. I was discussing this with Marci Davidson, my vice-principal at the time.

"We're going to need to pull a handful of students from each of the current third grade classes to form this new class," I lamented.

"How are you going to do that?" she asked. "Won't the parents be upset?"

"We don't have a choice. We need to contact parents and then we need to have teachers make recommendations for the students in the class. Students who are adaptable and not discipline issues."

"But, first we need to hire a teacher right?"

We made a plan for creating a new class and formed a team to conduct the interviews.

We narrowed it down to eight candidates. Janet scheduled all the appointments on one day and we secured substitutes for the teachers on the interview panel. The day went smoothly and we narrowed it down to three candidates we thought would be a good fit for our school and students. Now was the time to rank them and make a decision. I started the conversation.

"Candidate #3, Chris Strom, impressed me the most with her answers, but all through the interview I kept looking at her tongue piercing." This was the year 2001 and a tongue piercing was still unusual for our district.

"I know. I did too," commented Barry, one of our third grade teachers. "Do you think it would be a distraction for her students?"

"I don't know," I responded. "But I really liked the inclusiveness of her answers, and how she wanted to get to know her students and find out what each needed to be successful."

"I loved it when she said she liked to ask her students how effective a new teaching strategy was when she tried it."

"Yeah, I did too. I'm inclined to ignore the tongue piercing and take a chance on her. Chris knows her curriculum and should work well with our strong third-grade team. I think she would be a great asset to our school."

We hired Chris and she stayed at the school for many years as a very effective teacher in her own quiet way. She kept her tongue piercing and we never heard a student or parent mention it. She turned out to be one of our great bets.

~~~

In another instance we were hiring a vice-principal. Three schools needed VPs so we all interviewed together. There were eight candidates, four men and four women. They came in one at a time to answer our questions as we reviewed their resumes. One guy in particular impressed me with his mild-mannered approach. Nick Navarro was Latino, very soft-spoken but extremely thoughtful with his answers. After all eight interviews we huddled together in the room to discuss the candidates and which one each of us would like to hire. I had decided my choice was Peter and my only fear was that I would have to battle it out with another principal. Our district school population was about 45 percent Latino so to find a Latino male teacher was hitting the jackpot. To my surprise that battle didn't happen; no one else wanted to hire him.

"Well what did you all think?' asked our Director of Human Resources. "Does anyone have a choice right off the bat?"

"Yes," I eagerly responded. "I would like to hire Nick Navarro."

"Did you see that he answered 'yes' to one of the professional fitness questions about being convicted of a misdemeanor?" Pat Lyons, another principal, said. "I don't know that I would want him for a school vice-principal."

"Yes, I did, and I read his response explaining that answer. Apparently in college he was arrested for having an open container on campus. I thought about that in relation to my own two sons when they were in college. They didn't always make the right choices, but that didn't mean they weren't good people. Would I want them denied a job because of having an open container on campus? No. So I'm willing to take a chance on Nick. I liked his thoughtfulness regarding dealing with students."

I hired Nick and he was an outstanding vice-principal. He always dealt with students in a very inclusive and respectful manner. In fact, he later went on to become a VP at a middle school in our district and then an elementary school principal. He has remained in that position for ten years.

No PTA or Parent's Club!

*O*ne of the first things that comes to my mind when I think of elementary schools is PTAs and Parents' Clubs. These organizations have almost become synonymous with schools; kind of like salt and pepper or black and white. That partnership between schools and parents is crucial for a school to run effectively, so you can imagine my surprise when, on my first day as new principal, I had the following conversation with my office manager.

"Janet, could you get me the names and contacts of the PTA or Parents' Club officers?"

Janet gave me a blank stare and, not knowing her, I was trying to read what that meant when the light bulb went on, "Does that mean that there are no officers or that there is no PTA or Parents' Club?"

"Yep, both are right. We used to have one years ago but when the last principal was here, it stopped. I don't know why but parent attendance slowed down and when nobody did anything to regain interest, or have activities for parents, well then it just kind of disappeared."

"Oh wow! That's too bad. I'm really disappointed. Do we have any active parents who volunteer in the classrooms?"

"Yes, we have a few moms; there's Jessica Cooper, Alicia Magnini,

Lucy Garofino and Esther Jones. We also have a dad, Hank Hudson, who volunteers a lot."

"That's not many for a school of 720 students. Could you please contact them and set up a meeting to talk with me about starting up a parent's organization."

I walked back into my office bewildered. *Who helps the teachers in their classrooms and arranges for field trip drivers?* I had never considered that Baxter might not have a parent's organization. Actually, it shouldn't have been that much of a surprise to me. My very first teaching assignment had been at a small elementary school in Southern California where we didn't have a parent's organization either. That school had been about 50 percent Latino, a little higher percentage than the Latino population at Baxter. Many of the parents there didn't speak English and felt uncomfortable coming to the school. I suspected we might have the same situation here at Baxter. When I was teaching thirty years ago there were no English Language Development (ELD) programs for the students or English Learner Advisory Committees (ELAC) for the parents of second language learners. Nowadays schools are expected to have an ELAC if they have more than 20 English Language Learners at their school site. Hmm, I wondered if we had one here at Baxter. I went to ask Janet about that.

"Janet, do we have an ELAC here?"

"I think we're supposed to, but it isn't active. No one came to the last couple of meetings, so they stopped having them."

"Do we have a parent volunteer coordinator who reaches out to parents?"

"No, not anymore, we used to have someone but she retired and the former principal never replaced her."

I heaved a sigh and thought a moment. "What I'd like you to do is look at the calendar and find a date to schedule our first ELAC meeting. Then let all the parents of our English Learners know about it. Tell them I'm new and interested in meeting them and working together to support their students. We also need to find a Spanish speaking interpreter."

I could see the problem and the work that was cut out for us. Our school had a 45 percent Latino population and a 35 percent African American population, and it didn't seem there were any connections in place to make parents feel welcome. This would need to be a big focus of our school year and as I drove home that night I realized I was excited and eager to get to work and face the challenges ahead.

 "None of us is as smart as all of us." *~Ken Blanchard*

Family Literacy Night

*B*axter's first Family Literacy Night was an evening I will never forget. We had been waiting for months to share this occasion with our families. The atmosphere at the school was electric, with over 450 excited students and family members eager to attend the much-anticipated event.

Students were arriving through the big glass doors of the school lobby with their mothers, fathers, grandparents, aunts, uncles and siblings of all ages. Several teachers and I greeted everyone, and as every student arrived they were handed a booklet the teachers prepared describing the activities of the evening.

Students and their families were ushered into the cafeteria for a spaghetti dinner. The aroma in the room was much like an Italian restaurant with huge pots of spaghetti cooking on stovetops. The scent of fresh baked chocolate chip cookies wafted in the air. Families gathered together at the long tables, laughing and sharing stories with each other. Teachers wove in and out among the crowd, greeting students and parents.

Following dinner, students escorted their families out into the hallways where teachers staffed several literacy stations. They had spent weeks preparing materials for the variety of learning activities to be enjoyed by everyone, and were looking forward to sharing them with students and their families. As I walked through the halls I heard several comments from kids.

"Come over here Mama, we can make a book together."

"Papa, I helped my teacher figure out the words to use in this crossword game."

"Robbie, do you know what a synonym is?"

First-graders, just learning how to read, showed their parents how to make words with magnetic letters on cookie sheets. Fourth-graders created acrostic bookmarks out of construction paper, adorning them with glitter and feathers. Second-graders cut words from newspapers creating sentences and paragraphs demonstrating their newly learned skills. There was something for everyone and plenty of time for participants to wander from station to station.

Conversation bubbled among the visitors in anticipation of the appearance of our evening's mystery guest. When planning this event, Ann, a third-grade teacher, told us about a storyteller named Walter the Giant whom she had heard at another school. His name sounded intriguing, so we researched his website and immediately knew we wanted him to entertain at our First Annual Literacy Night. Luckily his calendar was open for this evening.

As seven o'clock approached we welcomed everyone back into the cafeteria, announcing on the PA system that our mystery guest had arrived. The crowd hurried to fill rows of seats at the long tables extending out from the side walls. As Walter the Giant entered the room gasps could be heard from the crowd.

"Oooo look at him, he's huge."

"He doesn't look like a storyteller."

"He looks like a lumberjack in those overalls and plaid shirt."

Walter was 6' 8" and carried about 300 pounds distributed evenly throughout his lumbering body. He had shoulder-length bushy hair, a full reddish-blond beard and a twinkle in his eye. Walter was a true storyteller; he sauntered up to the stage and immediately captured the audience with an imaginative story about Froggy getting ready for his first day of school.

Soon the audience was in stitches as Walter demonstrated how Froggy put on his socks, "Zip, Zip" and how Froggy put on his boots "Zup, Zup." Students from the crowd were brought up on stage to demonstrate with him a second time, "Zip, Zip," "Zup Zup." Pretty soon everyone in the audience was "Zip Zipping" and "Zup Zupping" with Walter. He spent the next hour entertaining everyone with funny story after funny story. When it was time for him to depart, Walter received a standing ovation. Our mystery guest had been an overwhelming success.

A buzz filled the hallways as Literacy Night ended, and students and their families left.

"This was the best night ever."

"Didn't you just love Walter the Giant?"

"Susie, I didn't know you knew how to read so many words."

"I hope we can do this again."

~~~

Our first Family Literacy Night at Baxter had surpassed our dreams. Everyone was leaving in good spirits and wanting more. We were proud of our school, and I was proud of our teachers who gave their time and energy to create a memorable evening for our students and their families. Before the night was over we were already planning our next Family Literacy Night.

 "Learning is not a spectator sport." ~*D. Blocher*

There is a Gun in our Garage!

*I*t was Thursday afternoon. Eddie was sitting on the bench in the office when I walked in after lunch recess. He was a first grader with curly, dishwater-blond hair and steely blue eyes. He looked at me with that guilty—*I know you said you didn't want to see me in here again unless it was for something good*—look. When he saw me he put a piece of paper over his eyes.

Janet handed me a note from his teacher, saying that at lunch recess Eddie had told three first-grade girls that he was going to come to school the next day and kill them. Oh my god! Eddie had done a lot of things before, but this hadn't been one of them. We were concerned about his behavior and had arranged for him to see Pam, our intervention specialist. That support had just started last week. I glanced at him sitting there sullenly.

"Eddie, come into my office. We need to talk."

Eddie got up slowly with his head hung down and followed me. We walked over to the tan wooden chairs next to the round table, and I motioned for him to sit down. He sat. I took the chair beside him and looked him in the eyes.

"Your teacher told me you told three girls that you were going to kill them. Did you say that?"

He looked at me and paused as if he was deciding whether to confess or make up a story.

"You know our agreement. You tell me the truth and I trust you."

"Yes, I told them I was going to kill them because they wouldn't let everyone play in their game. They were being mean and I was mad."

"So, you were upset because they wouldn't let you play in their game?"

"Yes," he whispered.

He stared at me for about ten seconds and I was astonished at what he said next.

"You know, I remember when I was little and my brother, or maybe it was my father, put a gun up on a high shelf in our garage. I wanted to get it, but it was really high up, and I was afraid of heights, so I didn't want to go that high." He stopped and looked at me. Then began to fiddle with some papers on the table.

A first-grader talking about guns and killing others! It caused me to retreat mentally, alarmed. I paused as his words sank in. *What would cause a 7-year-old to immediately jump to where he could access a gun? Was he thinking he could actually use it?* I made a note; this was something I would talk about with Pam and Andrea, our school psychologist. I spoke with Eddie some more and gently questioned him for extra details about the incident.

"Eddie, I need to make sure that you never tell anyone again that you will kill them. That's very inappropriate and frightens other people. Do I have your agreement?"

"Yes."

"You're going to have to miss recess tomorrow and I'm going to call your parents to let them know what happened today because I think it's important for them to know what you said. Do you understand?"

"Yes."

We ended our talk, walked back to his class, and I immediately went to find Andrea. Luckily, this happened to be one of her days on campus.

As I explained my conversation with Eddie, I could see by her furrowed brow that she was just as concerned as I was. We agreed to arrange a meeting with Eddie's parents as soon as possible; his behavior had been escalating and this was an alarming disclosure on his part. The touchiest part of the conversation was going to be telling them what he had said about the gun. My goal was for them to be aware of what was on Eddie's mind so, if they did have a gun, they could make sure that it was not accessible to their children. Also, I was hoping they would seek counseling for Eddie. I wasn't looking forward to that phone call.

By now school was out and I headed to Eddie's classroom to talk with his teacher. Before I called his parents I wanted her to know about my conversation with him. She was as distressed as I was.

"You know, he's been very hard on himself lately. He was mumbling 'stupid boy' under his breath this morning when he couldn't get the answer to a math problem and yesterday he threw his paper and pencil across the room when his drawing didn't turn out like he wanted."

"Have you talked to his parents about this?"

"I did call them last night. They said he'd not been getting along with his brother either so they would talk to him. They don't seem to want to be bothered with him, they have their hands full with the brother in middle school."

"Hmmm, good to know. I'm going to give them a call now."

I returned to my office. It had only been a few hours since I had seen Eddie, but it seemed like two days. I worried about what was going on with this little guy. However, at that moment I was focused on the phone call. I kept thinking about the best way to tell his parents. *If I were in their shoes what would I want to hear?* I felt it was best to be direct and just tell them what he told me.

"Hello, Mrs. McDonald," I began, "I need to talk with you about a situation with Eddie at school today." I explained what had happened and what Eddie said to the girls. Then I continued, "I am very concerned with what Eddie said next."

I proceeded to explain to her what he told me about his brother, his dad and the gun. She offered a few explanations. I told her we wanted to set up a conference with her, Eddie's father, our intervention specialist, the school psychologist, and his teacher. His behavior was escalating and we would like to meet as soon as possible.

She told me she had to work overtime this next week so could we schedule a date and time the following week. I couldn't believe she was so nonchalant about the situation. If someone called me to tell me my first-grader was talking about guns and killing others, I would be at school as soon as possible. Eddie was her third son. Her eldest son was thirteen and a handful. Maybe she had no energy left for Eddie.

That evening, I was looking forward to going to dinner and the theater with friends, but my mind was on Eddie. At dinner, my friends and I talked about kids in general.

"You know," said my friend, Maisie. "Kids are exposed to so much violence on TV and video games these days it worries me."

" I agree, and when these little ones have older siblings they get exposed to a lot more than most of their peers."

"It's hard as a parent to control what they see."

We arrived at the theater and I began to relax as I watched the play, a good distraction from real life. I could feel my shoulders lighten and the burdens of the day fall away as I laughed with my friends at the antics on stage.

Unfortunately, that unburdened feeling didn't last very long. My phone vibrated in my pocket. I looked down and saw a familiar phone number, then another message came in and another. It looked like Eddie's teacher, Paula had me on speed dial.

I waited until I could exit the theatre and then went out to the lobby to listen to the messages. Paula was trying to contact me to let me know the mother of one of the girls that Eddie had threatened wanted to meet in the morning.

So there I was at eleven at night, emailing a mother, assuring her that definitely I could meet her in the morning. Normally I would have followed my policy of waiting until daylight to contact a parent, but I knew my night's sleep, and hers, would be more restful if I made that connection before I went to bed.

The next day the girl's mother told me: "I'm very concerned about my daughter's safety. This isn't the first time I have heard of problems with Eddie. Other parents are concerned also"

"I understand. I can't discuss details regarding another student, but I can tell you we have talked with his parents and his teacher and we are watching him very carefully and putting support systems in place."

"Thank you. I appreciate knowing the school is taking this very seriously. I would also like to request that my daughter not be placed in class with Eddie next year."

"I'll make a note of that."

That afternoon we scheduled an SST meeting with Eddie's parents, his teacher, Pam and Andrea. We needed to get to the root of his behavior.

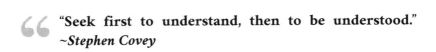

"Seek first to understand, then to be understood."
~Stephen Covey

Time for a Change

*S*ome people you always remember. They leave an imprint on your mind. Adeline was one of those people. She was the school librarian when I became principal. She had been there forever, was in her early seventies with closely cropped grey hair and always seemed to have a furrowed brow. In my first meetings with each teacher one concern I heard repeatedly was about the librarian. The teachers didn't feel that Adeline liked the students and said that she was always worried about them messing up the books.

I came from working at a school where the library was an interactive place. Kids pulled books off shelves, looked through them, and either put them back or decided to check them out. Plastic placeholders told them where to return the books. They might look through and read several before they decided which to check out. But that didn't happen in Adeline's library, mostly because that's exactly what it was: *'Adeline's Library'*. In her library the spines of books had to be aligned in a straight row. One book couldn't stick out farther than the one next to it. Everything in the room needed to look nice and neat. Consequently, students would take one book off the shelf and that would most likely be the one they checked out because, if they put it back and the spine wasn't straight, they would hear from Adeline.

"Excuse me, please go back and straighten that book out."

~~~

I remember the first staff meeting we held in the library. It made sense to me to hold it there; it was much roomier and more comfortable than the faculty lounge. At my former school we held all staff meetings in the library. I went to find Adeline to let her know the chosen date.

"Hmmm," she exclaimed with a surprise look. "Nobody checked with me to make sure that date was okay for a meeting."

"Oh was I supposed to?" I responded. "I checked the master calendar in the office and we had nothing going on in the library so I just booked it for our staff meeting and came to let you know."

"Its just that I've always given approval for any meetings held in the library."

Our conversation was a little crisp as I reminded her that the library belonged to the entire school and the staff meeting would be held after school, so it wouldn't conflict with student use.

"You know I don't allow any food to be eaten in the library?" she responded.

"Well, we do need to have some snacks and drinks. You know how hungry teachers are at the end of the school day. But don't worry, we'll be very careful."

"I really don't like to have food eaten in the library, it creates such a mess."

"Adeline, I understand your concerns, but teachers need to have snacks. Don't worry. You'll never know food was in here."

"Okay, but you won't be moving any tables and chairs will you?"

"I don't know for sure, but we might have to."

"If you do, I need you to move them back to their original places."

"No problem. We'll take care of that." I put my hand on her bony shoulder. "You'll never know we were in here."

She pulled a chair away from the table. "You see that spot on the rug where the chair was."

I looked down to see the small, round indentation from the chair leg.

"Please make sure all the tables and chairs are put back on those spots when you're finished."

I just looked at her and smiled. I wanted to say more, but I didn't. We ended the conversation and I walked away. I was shaking my head when I got back to my office. This woman was unbelievable; Baxter had a dictator as school librarian.

~~~

I began to spend more time in the library. I wanted to see first-hand Adeline's interactions with the students. I wanted to see what their experiences in the library were like. One afternoon I was observing her work with a fourth grade class. She was calling roll and students were returning books to her as their names were called.

"I don't have my book today." José said with his head down. "My mom was in a hurry to leave this morning and I left it on the kitchen table."

"Well, you'll need to go sit down and stay there until library period is over."

So José and a few other students who didn't have their books had to sit and wait until the end of their class library time, while the other students checked out their new books.

On another day I observed a fifth grade class as Adeline was taking roll and I was appalled as, one by one, she called out names, and when she got to Jésus (Haysoos as it is pronounced in Spanish), she said "Geezus" (as it is pronounced in the Bible). The young student offered, "My name is Jésus (Haysoos)." Adeline replied, "Why can't you pronounce it like it is supposed to be pronounced, like it is in the Bible?" Jésus just looked at her and then looked down at the floor. He

45

didn't say anything more. After roll call I went over and spoke to him privately. I made a mental note to talk to her about it later.

~~~

As the year went on we tried to get Adeline to change her library procedures. She made a few cursory changes, but it became obvious we needed a complete modernization. She just couldn't adjust to more inclusive ways of operation. What were we going to do? We needed a program that was inviting for students to explore literature and ideas. Our answer came in a most unusual form: technology.

Some of the libraries in the district had moved to automated systems. Ours had not made this leap and the staff and I felt it needed to be taken. I was pretty sure this idea wouldn't be well received by Adeline. Nevertheless, I approached her. As expected she resisted, saying things were fine the way they were, she didn't need to have the books entered into a computer, checking them out by hand worked just fine. She admitted she didn't know how to use a computer. I assured her we would send her to training, purchase the equipment needed, and give her all the support necessary to have the system up and running as soon as possible. Tears welled up behind her horn-rimmed glasses. She was genuinely fearful of making this big change. I felt badly for her. She had worked many years in the library and took ownership of what she felt was an organized, well-run system. Now it was being threatened. But we had a school full of students who needed a library that was responsive to their needs. We moved ahead with planning for the change to automation.

~~~

Midway through that year Adeline announced her retirement. She told me that she had been thinking for some time about this decision, had talked it over with her family, and felt it was time to spend more time with her grandchildren. I had mixed emotions about her decision, even though I knew it was best for our students. I felt badly for Adeline, but then again, maybe she just needed that little extra nudge of technology to cause her to make a decision she'd been thinking about for a long time. I gave her a big hug.

 "You must be the change you wish to see in the world."
~Mahatma Gandhi

The New Play Structure

*J*asmine sighed. The new play structure was beautiful! So much nicer than the old one, and it was even better than she had expected. The old one had been rusty, with some nasty, sharp places where she remembered getting too close and snagging her new shorts. This new one was smooth and shiny. It was Kelly green and bright blue. It was much bigger and had curves and corners going every which way. It was so new that we had to designate a time for each grade level to use it. Today was Monday, and it was fifth grade's scheduled turn.

Jasmine didn't know where to go first. She had waited so long for this moment. She was a fifth-grader on Student Council and they had worked together for months planning for this day. They had wondered what colors to choose.

"What color shall we make it?" asked Melanie.

"Bright red would be colorful and fun?" offered Rene.

"Could we have different parts of the structure be different colors of the rainbow, then everyone would have their favorite color?" joked Caroline.

"I think we should have it be the colors we see when we are outside playing on it," Lucas responded.

"That's a great idea," Jasmine agreed.

So they decided on Kelly green and bright blue to match the trees, bushes and sky outside.

Student Council had many discussions about what features they should select, there were so many to choose from. They had trouble deciding which ones would be best for the school so they created a survey and asked each student for his or her opinion. What did they want?

The students had been very engaged in the decision making process. It was exciting to see how thoughtful they were in their suggestions, each grade thinking of what older or younger students might want.

Jasmine was about to experience the results of all the Student Council's hard work and planning. She was now at the top and about to experience the one feature that all first through fifth graders said they wanted: she was ready to slide down the shiny, Kelly green, spiral slide on the top of our school's new play structure.

Perhaps I was as excited as Jasmine, recalling how awful and neglected the playground had looked on my first day at Baxter. I remember how disappointed I was seeing that tired, rusted structure with three sagging swings. It took a lot of lobbying with the district office to solicit some funds for a new one but, after several months of negotiating, we were finally able to move forward, creating an aesthetically pleasing and fun playground for our students. And the best part was how excited the students had been to be part of the selection process, making decisions such as whether they should have a straight slide, a curvy slide or both? Should they include monkey bars?

Participating in the creation of our new play structure helped Jasmine and the others develop a sense of pride and ownership in our school.

"Our" school, yes . . . . As I looked on I realized that I felt the same pride and sense of community as did the boys and girls around me.

Jasmine took my hand. "Come on, Mrs. Blomstrand. It's your turn!"

THE THIRD INNING

COMMUNICATION IS THE KEY!

Spider Webs

*S*pider webs are fascinating. They come in many shapes and structural designs. They can be beautiful, supportive, strongly connected, and yet look like works of art. They can also be messy, unstructured, destructive, and trap unsuspecting strangers in their undisciplined web.

Families are similar to spider webs. Most are strongly connected, supportive and provide a network for each other, but there are a few who are so unstructured they fall apart easily and pull their members into the web.

I thought of this analogy one day when Donnie was sent to my office. He was a wiry first-grader with dark brown hair and penetrating dark eyes who frequently had a scowl on his face. He didn't listen to adults well, didn't like being sent to the office, and was very quick to let us know his displeasure.

"I don't know why I'm here, I didn't strangle that girl!"

"Well. Then tell me what did happen."

"I just put my hands on her neck to scare her because she kept running into our game. I wasn't going to hurt her."

This was not the first time Donnie and I had conversations about his behavior. It had been a regular occurrence since kindergarten. In this situation I contacted his father to let him know what happened and made an arrangement with Donnie that for the next week he would help me and/or the custodian at recess.

Donnie's parents divorced just before he entered kindergarten. It was a contentious divorce and I had just learned that three months ago Donnie's father had obtained custody of the children; Donnie, his 8 year old sister and 13 year old brother. I know how hard it is in California for a father to get full custody, so I wondered what had happened. Donnie's web had changed dramatically and it was constantly vibrating.

One of the vibrations heard around the soccer field was that Donnie's father was in a year-long relationship with a woman who had two children at our school: a son in fourth grade and a daughter in second grade. According to the rumors, the two of them had recently moved in together with all five kids.

To complicate matters further, I also learned that last spring a Child Protective Services (CPS) report was filed charging the fourth-grade boy with sexually abusing Donnie. By the time we learned of this the case had already been closed. We don't know what the findings were, if there were charges, or if the accusation was unfounded.

~~~

Donnie's spider web was sticky and tangled. What could we do to help get it untangled? We needed to support him. I went to find Andrea Ogden, our school psychologist.

"Andrea, we just had another incident with Donnie Phillips. He put his hands around a girl's neck. He claims he only did it to scare her."

"What are you going to do with him?"

"I told him he would be spending recess either helping me or Rusty. I want him off the yard until we can put some steps in place to support him. He's hurting."

"That's good, I know he is, I think we need to call an emergency

SST. We need some counseling support for him and we need to talk with his dad."

~~~

We scheduled a meeting with Donnie's teacher, the school psychologist, his father, and we invited our district's Student Services Director to attend, she had many resources who could help Donnie and his family. We were looking for a cadre of folks who could untangle Donnie's web and stop it from vibrating.

At the meeting Donnie's father shared his struggles in raising his son as a single dad. We brainstormed together and established a plan of support for Donnie; weekly meetings with the school psychologist, weekly check-ins with the vice-principal and, Donnie's favorite was practicing his new skills by reading to kindergartners on a weekly basis.

 "When spider webs unite they can tie up a lion."
~Ethiopian Proverb

Project Read Volunteers

aisie and eight other people came from different businesses throughout the city: the steel factory, the school district office, the neighboring church, and a CPA firm. The one thing they had in common was their dedication to the students. They came for Project Read, a program sponsored by the County Office of Education. Reading with these first-graders was their passion and they arrived at school every Tuesday at 11:45 a.m.

Maisie and the others were volunteers who came to read to students or have the kids read to them. It always picked up my day when they arrived for I had never seen a group so consistently pleased with volunteering.

"Hey Maisie, good to see you. Who do you get to read with today?"

"I usually read with Cassandra. Do you know that when I started the program this year, she could only read three words, 'see, run' and 'dog?' Now she can read a whole book! You should see her. She glows when she's finished."

"You know it's huge for these kids that you guys come every week. That half-hour makes them feel really special and successful."

"Well, I'm glad, but, selfishly, I think I get more out of it than she does. When I walk into the library and see that smile cross her face when she sees me, it makes my day."

I received these kinds of comments every year from our Project Read volunteers. This was a community partnership that had a lasting impact on the lives of the students who were fortunate enough to participate and I only wished we had enough adults donating their time so we could provide help to every struggling first grader who needed it.

Just that morning I had engaged in a conversation with Paula, our first grade teacher who coordinated Project Read. We were discussing our end-of-year celebration for the volunteers and students.

"Jane, I've been thinking about how to get more people involved. You know the comments we hear each year from everyone about how much Project Read means to them. What if we put together a booklet with photos and comments? We could share it with Rotary and other service organizations to encourage more participation."

"Great idea! Wouldn't it be terrific if we ended up with more offers than we needed? We could expand to other grades. Let's do it!"

We talked more about Project Read and its impact on students.

"You know," I said. "Maisie was telling me she loves the personal connection she makes with each student she reads with; she feels they really get to know each other."

"I know," Paula responded. "I think it goes both ways because on Project Read Day the kids that participate can't wait to go read with their 'buddies'. That relationship they have built makes them feel so important and it's such a boost in self-confidence."

"It is isn't it? I don't think the volunteers ever completely realize how much listening to these students read affects their overall academic success."

I thought about Paula's idea of creating a booklet about Project Read. What a great way to share a valuable program with as many adults as possible. If we were able to reach more volunteers through our business and school contacts the possibilities could be endless.

Class Meetings

"Are we having a class meeting today?" Melanie—a fourth grader—asked as she bounded out of the classroom. "I sure hope so. I want to talk about what happened in the handball game yesterday."

"Yes, we'll have our meeting right after recess," replied Mrs. Rodriguez.

"Yay!" shrieked Melanie as she ran off to play with her friends.

~~~

After our staff discussions about building school community we had done some research and decided to institute class meetings. We had heard from staff at another school who said discipline issues for them had been reduced significantly since starting that procedure, so we discussed the idea and went to observe a similar school in Sacramento. After seeing their success we decided to hire the same consultant to train all of us. So far the process was working effectively.

When the recess bell rang, the students in Mrs. Rodriguez's class quietly lined up in single file on their room-numbered line in the playground. They waited for their teacher to come out and escort them to their classroom. You could hear a pin drop as they walked down the hallway to Room 25.

"OK, guys. Let's see how long it takes us to get into our Class Meeting circle," said Mrs. Rodriguez.

All students moved their desks to the side of the room, picked up their chairs, and almost like clockwork, each placed a chair in a circle in the middle of the classroom.

"One minute and 48 seconds, terrific! That is a class record. You guys keep getting better at this every day. Yesterday it was two minutes; today you beat that time by 12 seconds."

All the students in Room 25 got ready for compliments. That was how Class Meetings began.

Mrs. Rodriguez started with the student to her left. "Nicholas, do you have a compliment today?"

"Yes, I'd like to compliment Melanie because she helped me solve a fraction problem yesterday. I couldn't figure it out and she showed me the step I was missing. Thank you, Melanie."

Melanie beamed.

They continued around the circle with each student paying a compliment to someone else in the class for something they had done that showed they were practicing Life Skills. A couple of students didn't have a compliment, or couldn't think of one at that moment, and passed. Mrs. Rodriguez came back to them at the end of the round. Riley paid a compliment to Geraldo for showing him how to pump up the kickball. The look on Geraldo"s face said, *you just made my day!* You could tell that it made him feel really good. Actually, it was probably the first time he had ever received a compliment.

After compliments Mrs. Rodriguez looked at the Class Meeting Log. The first item on the list was one submitted by Tamika.

"Tamika, you wrote that you wanted to discuss a play structure incident this morning. Has that been resolved, or do you still want to discuss it?"

"We took care of that at recess so you can take it off the log."

"Okay, thanks, Tamika."

Mrs. Rodriguez went on to the next item. "Melanie, you wanted to discuss something that happened in the handball game yesterday. Is that still an issue?"

"Yes, Ellie and her friends play easy on each other so they can stay in the game, but they play really hard on everyone else. I don't think it's fair."

This started a discussion about the situation. Ellie had an opportunity to talk about her side of the story and defend her position. When the discussion ended, Mrs. Rodriguez asked the group for a resolution.

"What do you guys think? Is there any consequence that needs to be issued in this situation? Or do you think that it can be resolved by just not having it happen again?"

Ellie agreed that she and her friends would play fair with everyone, and the class agreed that if it happened again Ellie and her friends would sit out playing handball for one recess.

~~~

This was how it went at Class Meetings. When little issues were dealt with in an open and fair process they didn't grow into big issues. In this situation, Melanie had a venue to share her concern, Ellie had an opportunity to defend her side of the story, and the rest of the class acted as judge and jury. The criterion for consequences was simple—it had to be respectful, reasonable, and related to the event.

The Counseling Enriched Class

*O*ne day after lunch Wes came into my office. He sat down at the round table, let out a huge sigh, and put his head down on his folded arms, a very unusual gesture for this teacher. When he looked up his eyes looked watery.

"What's happening? Is one of the boys getting you down?"

"It's not one of the boys. It's Tanya."

"Tanya? But she worked up to Level 5 and she's been doing so well."

"I know, that's why I'm so upset"

Tanya was in Wes's Counseling Enriched Class (CEC) for students in third, fourth and fifth grades. She was in fifth grade, tall with dark brown eyes and brown hair, and was very athletic. She was known for talking back to teachers and getting into arguments with her peers. Wes and I had recognized a leadership quality in Tanya, but her behavior continued to get in the way of developing that talent.

The CEC had been designed for students who qualified for special education in the category of emotional disturbance. They experienced an inability to learn that couldn't be explained by intellectual, sensory, or health factors. These students had a very difficult time expressing their anger and frustration, and often would react by screaming, throwing furniture and attacking others physically.

Up until this year, students in our CEC had been receiving education in a specialized non-public school. When our district decided to open this class it was to provide a supportive environment for these young people to learn in, allowing them to return to public school. The class provided individualized education goals and counseling support. Students had to earn the right to participate in various activities in a general education setting. They did this by demonstrating the ability to express their frustrations appropriately. There were 5 levels and Tanya had earned Level 5, the highest, which meant she could have recess and lunch with the general education population of students. She loved joining her other friends on the playground.

~~~

As we talked, Wes stared out the window. "She was doing really well. She worked so hard to get to Level 5 and she was showing tremendous self-control. She was even helping some of the other students in our class and giving them strategies on how to control their tempers. And then at lunch recess today she lost it and got into a fight. Now she's back on Level 1 and has to start all over." Wes shook his head. "I try so hard with these kids and it's so frustrating when they blow it."

I understood his frustration. Wes's class was like a family. When students reached a new Level and earned another privilege, everyone celebrated. It was a big deal. It had been tough for Tanya to get through the process. She resisted the structure at first. When she finally realized the benefits of cooperation and teamwork she earned Level 5. Now she'd have to spend her recesses on the yard with Wes's class, at a different time than her other friends. She would be as upset about this as Wes. I looked out my office door into the waiting room.

"I see her now. She just came into the office with another girl. By the looks of the scowl on her face, I'll bet she's just as ticked off as you are. I know how proud she was to have her recesses with the other kids, and now she knows she's blown it."

Wes got up and looked out into the office. "Can we talk with her together? Do you have time to do it now before I have to go back to class?"

"Absolutely, you want to bring her in here?"

Wes had been teaching these students for over 20 years. He was well trained in diffusing potential blow-ups and putting positive behavior plans in place. He spent time getting to know the families of his students; he visited their homes and joked around with their brothers and sisters. These were the kids he wanted to teach; he'd do whatever he could to help them succeed in school and life. However, as caring as he was, he had high expectations for his students. He held them accountable for being in this class, the gateway for them to return into the general education setting. He wanted them to be prepared and they knew it.

We ended up talking with Tanya together.

"A group of us were playing dodgeball and Cecilia told me I was out when I wasn't. I tried to tell her what I did but she wouldn't listen to me, she just kept yelling 'you're out! You're out!' "

"So, then what happened?" asked Wes.

"She made me so mad and that's when I shoved her and she fell backward and hit her head on the pole."

As she talked tears rolled down her cheeks and she dropped her head to her chest.

" I don't know why I do those things, I just get so mad. I know I should count to ten or walk away, but sometimes I just forget what I'm supposed to do."

We talked some more, assuring Tanya that she could get back to Level 5 again; it wasn't the end of the world. We all make mistakes and the important thing is that we learn from them and move forward.

During the next few weeks Tanya worked very hard and with the support of Wes and the mental health therapists she earned her way back to Level 5. I saw her out on the yard playing with some of her friends. She saw me and gave me a thumbs-up, making me smile. I could tell how very proud she was of herself and what she had accomplished.

 "Students don't care how much you know until they know how much you care." *~John Maxwell*

Misperception

$\mathcal{Y}$ou can take your White racist ass back to your lily White suburb!"

Alice Anderson yelled those words at me as she stormed out of my office. I was speechless. I didn't know how to respond. I'd been called many things before, but never a racist. However, I couldn't stand there without saying anything because three fifth grade Black boys were in the office, staring at me wide-eyed . . . . I glanced over at them. They looked at me with that look that says, "What're you gonna do about that?"

I quickly searched for words. "I'm sorry you boys had to witness that. She was obviously upset and couldn't seem to find a better way to deal with her frustration." They smiled.

I hurried back into my office and immediately phoned the superintendent. I knew Mrs. Anderson would go directly to his office; she was a personal friend of his, a member of the local NAACP Board of Directors, and very influential in the Black community. He always liked a heads-up before an upset parent was headed his way.

"Don, you're about to have an angry parent in your office. Mrs. Anderson just left here in a rage because I suspended her grandson for hitting another student and I didn't suspend the other student who was White." I explained my encounter with her.

"What did the other kid do and what happened to him?"

"I benched him for a couple of recesses. I didn't suspend him because he didn't hit back. He verbally aggravated Bobby. He was teasing him, and Bobby has a short fuse and popped him in the face, gave him a bloody nose. You know how I feel about suspensions. I don't suspend unless it's a last resort, but when someone gets hit in the face, I think it's warranted."

"I know, I understand. I'll intercept her. I'm sure she'll be here any minute. I'll get back to you."

"Thanks, I appreciate that. Her words cut to the core."

"I know. I'll talk to you after I talk to her."

I leaned back in my chair. What now? The bell had rung and school was out, so I didn't have a chance to talk to the boys who had witnessed Mrs. Anderson storming out of my office. I felt as if I needed to follow through. I decided to call the boy's parents. I wanted to make sure their families knew the context of what had happened so hopefully there would be no misperceptions.

~~~

After calling the families I waited for the superintendent's return phone call. It seemed as if hours had passed. I was sitting on pins and needles. *What could be taking so long?* Finally, Don called me back.

"I think I have her calmed down. She understands why you made the decisions the way you did, but she would like to meet with you, Wanda, and me tomorrow morning. Are you available at 7:30?"

"Yes, I can be there. Do you know why she wants to meet?"

"I'm not sure. I think she just wants to clear the air. Don't worry; Wanda and I'll be there to support you," he said. "I'll see you in the morning."

~~~

That evening I agonized over the incident. I kept asking myself questions, most of them in the middle of the night when I should have been sleeping.

Could I have handled it differently?

Should I have handled it differently?

Knowing her grandson, Bobby, was Black and Josh, the other boy, was White, and knowing her involvement in the community, I anticipated there might be a problem, but should that have made a difference in how I handled the situation?

Was there something else besides suspension that could have been the consequence?

Why did it happen in the first place?

Why was Bobby so explosive?

Is there more we should be doing for him at school?

And finally, *what was this meeting about? Why did she want to have us meet with Wanda? Wanda Curtis was the Director of Student Services and responsible for all suspensions and expulsions in the district. Would Mrs. Anderson be bringing an advocate?*

After several hours of tossing and turning I finally went to sleep.

~~~

When I arrived at the district office the next morning I went straight to Wanda's office. Wanda was there, Don walked in right after me, and then Mrs. Anderson arrived with another gentleman. After nods and hellos we all sat down. Mrs. Anderson sat next to me and introduced me to her husband, Bobby's grandfather. She looked at me and slowly started speaking.

"I was so upset when I left your office yesterday that I came right down here to the superintendent's office to register a complaint. I was ready to take this case to the NAACP. Don and Wanda convinced me that you made a fair decision and I want to apologize for getting so upset and calling you a racist. That was very inappropriate of me. Please accept my apology."

"Thank you, I appreciate that. I don't believe I'm a racist so those words did bother me."

She turned to me and gave me a big hug. Mrs. Anderson had reacted based on her life experiences. We both had tears rolling down our cheeks.

I could feel my whole body relax. The incident caused me to reflect on how one's actions can easily be interpreted differently by others. I considered a favorite quote of mine by Steven Covey, *"Seek first to understand and then to be understood"* and reminded myself to post it on the wall of my office.

Student Success Assemblies

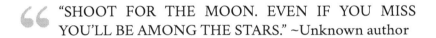

"SHOOT FOR THE MOON. EVEN IF YOU MISS YOU'LL BE AMONG THE STARS." ~Unknown author

*T*hat's what was written on the large poster hanging on the easel in the corner of the stage. I always loved that saying; I wanted the kids to know that trying your best makes you a star.

~~~

Today was a big day at Baxter Elementary. It was the last Friday of the month and the day of our monthly Student Success Assembly. The teachers put a lot of thought into which students they recommended for awards. Of course there were the traditional honor awards for grades, but we were trying something new this year. We were giving awards for the Life Skills we stressed at school so we had awards for Best Citizen, Most Responsible, Most Helpful, and Most Improved in Math, Reading, Writing, Science and Social Studies. These awards were particularly important because anyone in class who tried their hardest could be Most Helpful or Most Improved.

The atmosphere was electric as classes filed in the multi-use room and took their places at the long cafeteria tables. First graders sat in front on the floor. This was the first year for them to participate and you could tell by the buzz in the front of the room that they were excited. Older students chatted and waved to each other as they noticed their friends.

I was next to the stage greeting each class as they entered the room. Barry walked past as I was standing there.

"Well, Coach, are you ready?"

"I sure am," I said. "How do you like the poster? We made it this morning!"

He looked up at the stage and gave me a thumbs up.

The teachers looked forward to these assemblies as much as I did. It was an opportunity for them to acknowledge those kids who don't always receive positive feedback for their efforts, but make positive choices on a daily basis.

As I looked around the room my eyes landed on Anthony Baldwin. Anthony was in the fourth grade and just about as squirrelly as any little boy in the school. He was of average size, with big brown eyes, curly brown hair and always had a big smile on his face. However, Anthony rarely sat still to listen. His mouth was constantly getting him into trouble and he ended up in my office more than most of the other kids at the school. Still, there was something about him that I loved. He always expressed remorse when he did something he wasn't supposed to, and when he got into trouble it was usually for something like taking food from someone's lunch to give to one of his friends because his friend had forgotten his lunch. So he was a very caring boy. He just didn't make good choices.

Anthony was in Mrs. Vincent's room and his class was sitting about three tables back on the right-hand side of the cafeteria. As he turned around his eyes locked with mine and he gave me a big smile. Anthony was not one of the kids you would see walk up on stage at these assemblies to receive an award, but he was always clapping for his friends when they got theirs. I smiled back to let him know I saw him.

The assembly was about to begin. I went up on stage and welcomed everyone. I pointed to the poster and asked the kids to read it with me. We talked about the importance of trying our best and how that meant to "Shoot for the Moon," and how you never quite knew where your efforts were going to take you when you tried your very hardest.

We started the assembly with the first grade classes. Each teacher came up on stage and called out the name of the award and then the name of the recipient. The kids came up on stage one by one and stayed there until all names for their class had been read. I loved to watch their faces as they proudly walked up the steps. Some would look down at the ground, some would have funny little smirks, and then there was Jimmy Gonzalez, who quietly fist-pumped into the air. As each teacher finished handing out their class awards, we gave an enthusiastic round of applause and acknowledged everyone for their hard work.

Mrs. Vincent's class was next to be recognized. She came up on stage and began to read the name of each award and the student who was to receive it. When she got to the award for "Best Friend" she read the name Anthony Baldwin. Thrilled, I glanced over at Anthony. The surprised look on his face brought tears to my eyes. Anthony had a huge grin. He shot out of his seat, ran down the aisle and bounded up onto the stage to greet Mrs. Vincent. Everyone could hear him as he said, "Thank you, thank you, thank you. This is the best day of my life!"

 "It's a funny thing about life; if you refuse to accept anything but the best you very often get it." *~W. Somerset Maugham*

Was It Really Vandalism?

*Y*ou never know what you are going to find when you arrive at school on a Monday morning. Public schools are just that—public—which means anyone can use the school grounds when school is not in session. That use is usually limited to organized soccer and baseball games, and parents and kids enjoying the swings and the slides.

But that is not always the case, as I discovered one Monday morning when Rusty, our custodian, came into my office.

"Bad news this morning, boss. It looks like we had some partying over the weekend. Whoever it was broke the tent the district erected in front of the new kindergarten portables, and I found a broken "marijuana bong" on the sidewalk nearby. I have pictures of all of the damage; you can see where the tent poles are all broken near the bottom. It looks like they kicked them in or something. Take a look."

"Oh jeez!! Have you talked with Tim yet?" Tim Esposito was head of maintenance for the district. "We need to take a look at the surveillance cameras to see if they show anyone on campus over the weekend. Have you had a chance to clean it up yet?"

"Not yet, I'm headed back over there now. Just wanted to let you know. I don't know how to view the cameras. We'll need to have Mark over in technology come to do that."

"OK, let's go look. Then you go ahead and clean it up and I'll contact Tim and Mark."

When I returned to my office I sat down and took a deep breath. This was the part of the job of being a principal that frustrated me. I had planned on conducting classroom visitations this morning, and now I had to spend time dealing with this vandalism issue, which had nothing to do with instruction and learning.

But these kinds of issues had to be taken care of immediately. It didn't really matter what the plan for the day was. First I needed to notify the superintendent. It was important for him to know when anything unusual occurred on campus. I wasn't surprised when he asked me to make sure to notify the police.

Okay, first Tim, then Mark, because they needed to take time out of their schedule to get over here. Then I would phone the police.

~~~

My conversation with the police sergeant was very short. He wanted to know what we had seen on the surveillance cameras, so I agreed to phone him back once I knew.

Mark was very helpful when he arrived. He showed me how to open the cameras and navigate my way through the maze of photos. We were perusing all the different locations in the school where cameras were positioned when Ben returned to my office.

"Have you seen anything suspicious?" he asked.

"Not yet, there really isn't much activity, come take a look. We have lots of surveillance cameras but don't have one positioned on the portables where the damage occurred."

It was fascinating viewing film of the different locations on campus. There was a man walking his dog, a woman in the hallway outside the first-grade classrooms sitting at a table eating her lunch. We saw what looked like a mother and her two young kids swinging on the swings, and a boy about eleven or twelve years old walking across the playground. Other than that the campus was very quiet. I made a note to ask the district to install another camera on the section of the yard where we had two new portables.

Right then Tim walked in. He had been out inspecting the damage our partygoers had caused and walking the school to make sure we hadn't missed anything.

"Well, I solved what happened. I'm sure the tent blew over because of that high windstorm blowing through here Saturday night. The poles are all bent at the same place. That tent should have been secured with sand bags around the base of each of the support poles but it wasn't, so when the wind came whipping through it just lifted that tent up and slammed it down, breaking the poles."

We all looked at each other and laughed. I felt a little stupid that I hadn't thought to ask that question earlier, knowing that we'd had some strong winds over the weekend, but the broken bong had convinced me that the midnight revelers did the damage. We will never know exactly what happened but not enough evidence existed to warrant further investigation.

I phoned the police sergeant back to let him know we didn't need a police report after all and then updated the superintendent. All of that sleuthing had taken an hour and half, just the same amount of time I had allotted to conduct my classroom visitations. Still, it was good to uncover the truth.

Construction

School modernization as a process has its yin and yang. The yin is that the campus is disrupted during the process, classes are relocated, walls are torn down, and there is noise, dust and chaos everywhere. The yang of the process is that you end up with new, beautiful, and hopefully more functional school buildings. According to Chinese philosophy these forces are actually complementary and interrelated.

When Baxter went through modernization we definitely experienced both yin and yang. Our school was comprised of five building wings and six portable classrooms. Each wing contained four classrooms. We had meetings with architects and builders and gathered input from the teachers about their wishes for cabinets, flooring, etc. After gathering information from the staff and the school district, architects and builders made decisions regarding details of construction.

I was asked to attend the first of the construction meetings. Here actual plans for the process took shape. Our district Director of Maintenance attended, as well as the team from the contracting company. I listened as the Construction Manager explained how they would relocate classrooms during the building process.

"What we plan to do is place two portable classrooms on the playground. Then we can move half the classes at a time out of each wing. We can do the construction on the two empty classrooms, then move those classes back into their rooms and the other two out. We'll do this with each wing until we're finished."

I thought to myself, *you're going to keep two classes in the wing with all that hammering and dust flying around. That's crazy; kids can't learn in that kind of chaos.* "May I ask a question? "

"Sure, Jane."

" Could you put four portables on the playground? Then you'd be able to move all classrooms out of the wing at once. You'd have the whole wing to yourselves and it would be faster and more efficient than having to work around two classrooms full of students."

A long discussion then ensued about the cost of four portables versus two, disruption on the playground, timing, etc. The group finally agreed that it would probably take less time with all classrooms out of each wing when construction was going on; therefore it made sense to put four portables on the playground.

Whew, I thought, and decided then and there that I needed to attend each one of these weekly construction meetings, even though they would be held throughout the summer. An educator's voice needed to be heard when decisions were made, someone who understood the perspective of what happens on a school site.

~~~

The actual building was the yin part of the modernization process. Living through the chaos was challenging. Being on top of the process through all steps along the way took many hours and pulled some of my focus away from curriculum. But in the long run it paid off. Our teachers took charge of instruction, and I took charge of making sure we came away with what we wanted for our school. Teachers and staff were wonderfully patient and resilient during the process. Every few months we moved four classes out to the portables, and four classes of students moved back into their new, modernized classrooms. Everyone seemed to understand that you could put up with the yin knowing you would get the yang as the reward. They loved their new classrooms!

Even though it was disruptive during construction we managed to have some fun. Halloween came in the middle of the modernization, and several teachers thought it would be cool if we all dressed up as construction workers. We ordered hard hats for all staff with "Baxter Elementary Construction Crew" on the front. The students enjoyed seeing us walk around all day with our work belts filled with hammers and screwdrivers. It definitely broke the tension of the situation and created a bond as we laughed and commented on whose construction belt held the most unusual tools.

Another yang of the process occurred at one of our Leadership meetings when Francie, one of our fourth grade teachers asked a question.

"Jane, you know how we have such a big focus on Life Skills at Baxter? I was at a friend's school and saw a tile wall created by students. Since we're all torn up anyway could we create something like that here? The students could paint tiles depicting different Life Skills."

That comment started a wave of discussion with ideas igniting throughout the room. Where would we put it? Would all the kids participate? What would it look like? Would the builders be able to install it? Would we be able to organize an event for students to create their tiles in time to have it installed? Thoughts flew. I agreed to ask at the next construction meeting if this could be possible and asked Tim, our Director of Maintenance to put me on the agenda.

"The teachers are very happy with how the new tile looks on the hallway walls," I told the group. "We had a discussion at our last Leadership Team meeting and we have an idea that we want to ask you if it would work? "

I proceeded to tell them our idea about creating a colorful, tile wall of Life Skills created by our students. That prompted an interesting discussion; the construction group actually seemed very excited about this happening.

"Do you know where you would want to place the Life Skills wall?" asked Tim.

"Well, we were thinking in the lobby where everyone could see it every day if that's possible. It could be a constant reminder of how we treat one another at Baxter and what is important to us like cooperation, responsibility, and respect." I responded. "There's that big wall right across from the office and I was thinking since the new tile only goes half way up the wall that maybe we could construct our Life Skills wall above that."

"Tell us again exactly what would go on this wall?" asked Bill, the Construction Superintendent.

"It would be six inch tile squares that have been hand painted by our students, as many as could fit in the space provided as well as a heading, something like "BAXTER LIFE SKILLS". I don't know yet because we haven't created any of it yet. But the tiles would be the same size as the new tile you are installing on the walls."

"That would be good. You know we are on a construction schedule and we can't hold that up. Could you get the tiles painted and ready to be installed by February?" asked Bill.

"Absolutely! I think this will be an excellent finish to the whole school construction project, one that we all can be proud of helping create."

~~~

Planning began on the process. We had to move fast and stay on schedule. We developed a flyer to send home to parents with details of the process. Students could choose one of our school's Life Skills and create a pattern for how they wanted to represent it on their tile. They would bring their design to the tile-painting event we would plan and create their own tile. The students were excited and delighted in planning and preparing for what they would actually paint.

The tile-painting event occurred on a Saturday with hundreds of students and their families crowding into the school multi-use room. We worked with a company who specialized in this kind of product so they guided each student through the process.

The end result was a beautiful 25' by 8' wall of colorful hand painted tiles representing our school's ideals, and we would all see it every day as we walked into the lobby. I'm not sure who was more excited, our students or the construction crew. A definite yang to the construction process!

 "Experience is not what happens to you; it's what you do with what happens to you." ~*Aldous Huxley*

My Daughter Was Sexually Assaulted!

*I*t was my mistake to check email at 11:00 on a Friday night. I was visiting my son and his family, and was just about to lay my head down on the pillow when I saw I was copied on an email message from the father of one of our students. It was addressed to his fifth grade daughter's teacher, Lynn Vander.

Dear Ms. Vander, what are you going to do about the fact that a male student sexually assaulted my daughter today at the music performance on the school campus?

~~~

Was I reading this right? I read it again. Did the father of a fifth grader just accuse another student of sexually assaulting his daughter? At a fifth grade music concert? I hadn't been on site that day so wasn't aware of what happened. Surely Lynn would have notified me if sexual harassment had occurred. But what did happen to cause such an accusatory email?

I didn't know the father who was sending this email so, wanting to learn more about him, I went to the Internet and discovered that he was an attorney for a large public relations firm. Now he was accusing a fifth grade boy of sexual assault? What had his daughter told him? I assumed he didn't yet know all the details of the incident. Why was he using such inflammatory language? I couldn't imagine how this could have occurred. Had this father just consumed a little too much soda pop on a Friday night and not filtered his message?

I emailed Lynn and she responded right away. The girl had come to her right after the music concert at the end of the school day and told her about an incident in the multi-use room. The kids were sitting in the bleachers listening to a music concert, when one of the boys in class had touched her bottom. She reported this as the students were walking out of class to go home for the weekend. Lynn hustled out to the exit area to look for the boy but he had already been picked up. She then phoned both sets of parents to let them know about the incident and told them we would conduct an investigation on Monday morning.

I chose not to respond to the father's email at eleven at night. His message was inappropriately written and if I responded mine might sound equally offensive. Better to sleep on it. The next morning I emailed, advising him that I had received his message and would investigate the incident on Monday morning. I alerted our superintendent just so he would be aware of the accusation: he always appreciated a 'heads up' in case he might receive a phone call.

On Saturday morning Lynn called to give me more details about what happened.

" Lynn," I assured her. "You did the right thing. You notified both sets of parents right away and told them we would be looking into the situation first thing Monday morning."

"Thanks, I wanted to make sure they heard what I knew about the incident from me because I was sure they would hear from their kids about it. In fact after I received that email from Susie's dad I called Kevin's parents again. Kevin's father's response was "Why didn't

Susie's dad just call me, and we could have straightened it out together with our kids. He and I know each other."

Over breakfast I reflected on that comment with my son. We remembered many of the issues when he was young, and recalled how parent intervention had helped solve many an incident.

~~~

Monday morning rolled around and we started the day looking into what had happened. I asked the school psychologist to sit in on the interviews. One by one we called students into her office, starting with the victim, Susie.

"Good morning, Susie. I understand something happened at the music concert last Friday, can you tell me about it?"

"Well, we were standing up, listening to the music and clapping our hands, and all of a sudden Kevin touched my butt."

"Can you show me exactly what he did?"

She brushed her hand against her bottom.

"Did he say anything when that happened?"

"No, I turned around and he just looked the other way."

"Do you think he did it on purpose?"

"I don't know."

"Were there any other students who saw what happened?"

"Yes, Sophia and Charlie, they were both right there."

After about two hours of investigation, talking to many students, the story was obvious. The students were clapping their hands to the music. Kevin was in the row behind Susie and, in the process of clapping, one of his hands brushed against her bottom. When she turned around he looked the other way and didn't say anything because he was embarrassed. The kids, including Susie, were all in agreement that it was an accident and no harm caused. That was it!

We phoned all parents and notified them of the results of the investigation, and they all seemed satisfied with the outcome. We tried to talk with Susie's father directly but he was never available, although

I did talk with her mother who thanked the school for taking so much time to investigate.

I never heard anything from Susie's dad. Not an, *"I'm sorry I jumped to that conclusion."* Nothing! In our society it's easy to shoot-off an angry communication expressing concerns.

I frequently talk with my peers about how thoughtful we need to be when delivering those messages. It's a two-way road as we work with parents. There are a small handful of people, like this dad, who drive on the wrong side, causing unnecessary havoc for others. Fortunately, 99 percent of our parents and teachers flow well together as they travel down the highway.

Spirit Days

---

*E*very month when we held School Spirit Day the kids came to school in all kinds of attire and hairdos! Each time we waited in anticipation for the next student to arrive, marveling at the creativity they displayed.

Two months ago "Crazy Hair" day had amazed me! I was standing in front of the school when I saw Lakisha. Her black, curly hair was in a ponytail sticking straight out of the top of her head. She had a fuzzy green ribbon tied around it. When she saw me she was laughing so hard she could hardly contain herself. Her smile spread from cheekbone to cheekbone.

"Wow! That's some hairdo, Lakisha. How'd you get it to stand up like that?"

"First my mom put my hair in the ponytail. It was hard because it's so curly. She had to keep pulling it out straight. Then she took hair gel, slopped it all over the ponytail and held it straight up 'til it dried. It just stayed there. I hope it doesn't fall over. I want to win the contest."

I thought Lakisha would win for sure, but then I saw Ramona. She had a braid sticking straight out of each side of her head. Yellow curly ribbons were dangling from the end of each one. She came prancing into school as if she was walking down a Paris runway.

"Look at you, Ramona. I love your hairdo, did you do that yourself?"

"No, my two sisters helped me. Each one took a side at the same time. They covered my hair with gel and braided it starting from the top of my head. Then they tied these curly ribbons around it and held it straight out until it dried."

Hairdo after hairdo came through the door, each one unique and unusual, from Mohawks to 10 braids sticking out of one head. It was difficult to judge the "Crazy Hair" contest. We ended up giving many different kinds of awards, most for creativity.

~~~

Last month, School Spirit Day was Twins Day. We couldn't wait to see what creative attire the students would enter the door wearing. Two second-graders, Brittany and Carlotta, arrived first. They bolted out of the bus doing that "fast walk" kids do to get to the door first when they're not supposed to run. Both were dressed in blue jean overalls rolled up to their knees, with red, yellow and orange striped shirts. Both of them had one fluorescent orange knee sock and one fluorescent yellow knee sock. They wore red tennis shoes on their feet and bright red grosgrain ribbons tied in their ponytails.

"You guys look adorable; your outfits are so bright and cheery. You look like matching bookends. I love it!"

They smiled, looking down at the ground, their faces turning red. "Thank you," they mumbled.

Right behind them emerged a bubbly group of fifth grade girls, laughing and chatting. All ten of them were dressed in blue jeans, white short sleeved t-shirts, tennis shoes, ponytails with purple ribbons, and yellow bandanas tied around their necks. These girls were excited about the day. "Are we having a contest today for the best outfit?"

"We sure are, but it'll be tough for the judges to choose. You guys have been so creative." They hurried off to their classrooms.

~~~

The staff all began to look forward to these days, mostly because the kids looked forward to them and participated with such enthusiasm.

The third Spirit Day, "Pajama Day," found most of the teachers out front in the school lobby waiting for the first students to arrive when the coolest thing happened. Three teachers came walking down the hall, all dressed in pajamas. Paula, a first grade teacher, had big fuzzy pink slippers on her feet. Chris, who taught third grade had fuzzy slippers shaped like teddy bears, and Barry of course had Mickey Mouse slippers on his feet. They were all wearing bathrobes and Paula was even carrying a 'blankie.' The kids loved it and the rest of us laughed hysterically.

~~~

I loved the fact that the teachers were now getting into the excitement of our Student Council sponsored "School Spirit" days. Whether it was "Crazy Hair Day," "Twins Day," "Pajama Day," or Sports Day," it was a special event. Teachers and students participated together, adding to a very positive school culture.

66 **"It is good to have an end to journey toward; but it is the journey that matters in the end." ~*Ernest Hemingway***

THE FOURTH INNING

LIFE IN A SCHOOL IS NEVER BORING!

The Parent Volunteer Coordinator

*I*t was 2:45 p.m. when the parents started arriving. Cookies, fruit and water had been set up on the front table in the school library. We had prepared information packets for everyone and stacked them neatly on the corner of the table. It was the first English Learner Advisory Committee (ELAC) meeting of the year, and the first one held at the school in a long time, according to Janet, our office manager.

The State of California required all schools with more than 20 English Learner students (ELs), to establish an ELAC and communicate with parents. At last count we had almost 150 EL students and no existing committee. The school had been completely out of compliance for quite awhile.

I had worked with Juanita Ferris and Rosaria Garcia two of our instructional assistants, to plan this meeting. Juanita was the person at Baxter who was called on to translate for parents when needed and she spoke just enough Spanish to communicate an important message. The three of us had discussed significant topics and meeting logistics. We wanted a casual, friendly atmosphere and kept going back and forth on how to arrange the room to make it welcoming.

"Let's have small tables of four to five people. It seems intimate that way."

"I was thinking we could have everyone sit around one table facing each other. We only have 15 RSVPs and it may be friendlier that way."

We ended up deciding on one long table so we could all see each other, and had the custodian set up the room that way.

~~~

Ten minutes before the meeting, 25 people had already arrived and more were gathered outside. Yikes, our one table wouldn't hold everyone. We went back to the small tables. We quickly rearranged the room.

Most of those arriving were mothers, with just a couple of dads. They were all very polite and smiled at us, nodding as they walked into the room, many pushing baby strollers. Occasionally someone would thank me for having the meeting and say they had been looking forward to it, but most didn't say anything.

We greeted each of the parents as they entered and let them know we had child care down the hall. After talking with each other, most parents sent their kids down the hall, except the toddlers who were reluctant to leave.

Luckily we had anticipated the need to have childcare available, which was good because most of the parents did bring their children. It was so different from my former school where, if we held a parent meeting, everyone secured sitters at home.

Rosaria had set up a nearby classroom with art supplies, games and books, to entertain the kids who showed up.

People seemed very upbeat. The room buzzed as folks chatted with one another while getting their snacks and sitting down. As I listened I became aware that most of the conversations were in Spanish.

Once folks were seated, Juanita and I introduced ourselves and welcomed everyone.

"I'd like to go around the table and have everyone say their name and what grade(s) their children are in."

A young mother quickly went first. She was tall with shiny black hair, laughing brown eyes, and a beautiful smile. I could tell by how the other parents gravitated toward her that people felt very comfortable with her.

"I'm Neri Aceves and I have a son in kindergarten and a son in second grade."

The other parents followed in turn. I watched this young mom. She seemed very in tune with those around her and I noticed her many times in short, whispered conversation with others.

We talked about the EL programs in the district, the English proficiency test that all their children would take, the purpose of this group, and how often we would meet. It was a short meeting, ending an hour after we started. A few parents thanked us for holding it, but most just smiled, nodded, and quietly left.

The young mom lingered after the rest of the parents were gone. "I would like to introduce myself again. My name is Neri Aceves. I have two boys at Baxter, kindergarten and second grade. I know a lot of these parents. If you are interested, I would be happy to offer my services at these meetings. Most of these parents don't speak English and I would be pleased to translate for you."

"Thank you so much. You just answered a question for me. How many would you say are non-English speakers?"

"At least three quarters of the room."

"Wow, no wonder most of them just smiled at me and nodded. I can't believe I didn't think about that. That was insensitive of me. Is it typical for the Latino parents to bring their children to meetings like this?"

"Oh yes, most of these folks can't afford babysitters. They go everywhere as a family, unless, of course, they have a family member to stay at home with their children, but many don't, particularly in the daytime. They very much want to be part of their child's school; they just have never been included here. That's why you had such a big turnout. They figured someone would be here who spoke Spanish and could help them understand how to get more support for their children."

~~~

Within a month I hired Neri as Parent Volunteer Coordinator. The first thing she did when she set up her office was to hang a sign that read, "You bet your tortilla I'm Mexican." I loved it and so did the parents. She translated all of our homebound materials into Spanish and represented parents at all of our SST and ELAC meetings. In fact Neri became an important link between our school and the Latino community. It also began a very long association and friendship between the two of us, which has lasted until this day.

 "Coming together is a beginning, keeping together is progress, working together is success." *~Henry Ford*

I Didn't See the Orange Tip!

*W*hen I arrived at Baxter, several people warned me about Peter. He was described as a kid who disobeyed authority, bullied other students, and had difficulty academically. I was told he terrorized the playground and persuaded other boys to join in his antics. He had been a weekly visitor in the office.

My first encounter with him came the second week of school. He was sent to me because of a playground incident. Peter was 11 years old, tall for his age and slight of build. He had curly light brown hair, blue eyes and an engaging smile. He was outgoing and charming, eliciting conversation the moment he walked into my office. He was a charismatic young man.

"I can explain everything, Mrs. Blomstrand," he began as he entered. "It wasn't what the yard duty thought it was." Peter talked quickly while anxiously pacing back and forth.

"Really? Take a seat and tell me in your words what happened."

That began the first of many conversations and encounters Peter and I had in my office. We developed a good relationship. The more I learned about his background and his learning disabilities, the more I recognized his need to prove himself. He wasn't one of the most athletic students on campus and academics were very challenging for him so he found that by defying authority his peers gave him lots of attention. We kept trying to find something that would give him more positive feedback. I remember one conversation with Peter that may have been the start of the turnaround in his behavior.

"Peter, I saw you in the library at lunchtime today. "

"Yeah, somebody told me they had board games in there for kids to play during recess."

"Oh right. Our new librarian started that. Was it fun?"

"Yeah, kind of. Some kids were playing checkers but I saw another game like checkers. It was called chess, it looked like fun."

"Oh it is, would you like to learn how to play chess?"

"Yeah."

I shared that conversation with his teacher, Donna Johnson, and she taught him how to play chess. He became very good at the game. He came to realize his great talent for strategizing about moves to capture his opponents. He was becoming recognized among his peers as a chess genius. Slowly but surely, Peter became less of a fixture in my office. His behavior in the classroom and the yard improved.

So it was disconcerting when this call came into my office one morning at 11:00.

"Jane, you need to get down to Donna Johnson's classroom. One of her students just hit her."

I quickly called Pam, our school intervention specialist, and asked her to meet me in the classroom. When we arrived, Donna was sitting on the floor holding Peter in front of her in a bear hug, her arms folded across his chest, and her legs wrapped around his legs. His backpack was lying on the ground next to them. Her two teaching assistants were standing over them. The rest of the students were quietly sitting at their desks, eyes glued to their teacher and Peter. I looked at the teacher.

"Donna, Are you OK?"

"Yes, I'm fine, just a little shaken up."

I asked the teaching assistants to take Peter down to my office and call his family. Pam went to talk with the other students and I went into the classroom office with the teacher. She was visibly shaken and breathing hard, but she relaxed back in her chair.

"Are you sure you're okay?"

"Yes, I'm not hurt. He didn't hit me that hard; he only slapped my arm." A tear rolled down her face. "I'm just upset about the whole incident and that it was Peter."

"What in the world happened?"

"We were just finishing our math lesson when I noticed him whispering with another student. Peter was pointing to his backpack under the table and before I could say anything he reached into it and pulled out a black handgun. I didn't hesitate. I ran over and grabbed his hand to pull it off the gun and keep him from pulling it out further. When I grabbed his hand he slapped me on my arm and screamed at me to let go. My aides saw what was happening and ran over and grabbed Peter. He dropped the weapon and tried to wrestle away from them. I shoved his backpack away from him and the other students with my foot, and the three of us wrestled him to the ground where I put him in the bear hug."

"What a terrifying experience!" I was trying to process the whole incident.

"It all happened so fast. It wasn't until we had him on the ground that I could see the gun lying next to his backpack and noticed the orange tip on the end of the barrel. It wasn't even a real gun. Until then I had no clue that it wasn't the real thing. They look so much alike. I can't believe he brought it to school after all the discussions we've had. He knows better." She sighed. "He has been doing so well. What happens now?"

We were both thinking the same thing. Our school district had a zero-tolerance policy about students bringing weapons to school, and/or assaulting a teacher. Violation of these policies caused an automatic recommendation for expulsion. What would that mean for Peter? After he had made such great improvements, would we have to expel him?

~~~

We suspended Peter for five days, as district policy dictated. That allowed us to investigate the incident, hear from Peter, interview all witnesses, and then make a decision at his expulsion hearing. We were concerned as we talked about Peter's academic future at the hearing.

"So, if we expel him what does that mean?" I asked. "Will he be out of school? That's not best for him. But he hit a teacher and that's not okay either."

"We can look for alternative placements for him, there are non-public school options available but we need to see if they have openings for a fifth grade boy."

Our student services director did some research and we found an alternative school placement for him in a non-public, small school setting where we all felt he would have more chance for success.

~~~

There are students like Peter in schools everywhere. How do we support their needs and keep everyone safe? Schools have to put systems in place that support students like Peter while, at the same time, providing for the security of all students and staff.

 "The kids who need the most love will ask for it in the most unloving ways." *~Russell Barkley*

Surprise on the Trail

*T*he kindergarten teachers heard a racket outside the classrooms and several frightened 6-year-old girls rushed into the room, many of them crying and all of them talking at once.

"We need help," hollered Amanda.

"Mrs. Jenkins was hit and she's hurt," cried out Tiffany.

"We were just hiking and it came after us," screeched Sophia.

"She's coming down from the trail now, she's right outside."

"I think we need to call a doctor."

At that moment Mrs. Jenkins stumbled into the room, her face was white and she looked to be in shock. Another mother was holding her waist and guiding her to sit down, and several more girls were right behind them, some crying, and some just talking very fast trying to tell the story of how Mrs. Jenkins got injured. The teachers rushed to her side.

Mrs. Jenkins, clutching her arm said, "I'm okay, it's just a bump, I'm okay girls, don't worry."

However, to the group of teachers huddled around her as she shifted back and forth on her feet she said, "I don't want the girls to hear me but it hurts so much if I stop moving I think I'm going to faint."

The teachers, seeing 8 hysterical girls and several moms who were almost as hysterical, sprung into action. One teacher got popsicles for the girls and invited them to a corner of the kindergarten room to settle them down with a story. Another rushed to the office to get ice for Mrs. Jenkins and let me know what was going on, and a third stayed with the mothers, comforting them and trying to find out just what happened.

She learned that the girls met after school with their Girl Scout "Daisy" Troop. The Daisies are the kindergarten Girl Scouts and they meet every Wednesday on the yard after dismissal. Mrs. Jenkins and another Mother were the Troop leaders.

On this warm and sunny day the leaders decided it would be fun to take the girls on a hike in Brandman Park, right next door to the school. There was a wonderful hiking trail through the park, not too steep with lots of natural vegetation; it would make a great nature hike. Perfect for these 6-year-old Daisies. They finished their picnic lunch and, after selecting partners—because in girl scouts you always hiked with a buddy—they started off on their trek.

The Troop leader's daughter, Amanda Jenkins, was in the lead. Amanda loved to run and relished the attention when others followed her. A group of girls ran ahead with her and as they rounded the corner of the trail, they spotted a small group of cows about a block away. They stopped in their tracks. It wasn't like the girls had never seen cows before but on this day, in this setting; the three older cows and little calf looked so peaceful and happy just grazing on the grass. The girls were admiring them when the rest of the Troop rounded the corner. Amanda hollered to her Mom.

"Can you take our picture with the cows?"

"Well not with the cows, but we can take it with the cows in the background," Mrs. Jenkins told them. "Come on over here, everybody get in the picture. Move back a little, get just a bit closer but not too close."

The girls scrambled to get in the front of the photo when all of a sudden one of the cows charged the group. Everyone ran, screaming but the cow was quick and knocked down Mrs. Jenkins. She couldn't get out of the way fast enough causing a domino effect knocking over three girls.

Pandemonium broke out with girls crying and running, and mothers, upset themselves, trying to calm down the girls and get them away from the cow. They managed to herd the girls to safety and the cow ran off snorting.

The kindergarten teachers listened in astonishment as the girls and mothers told the story. They never heard of a cow charging people but apparently a calf was involved so it seemed the mother cow was just being protective of her baby.

"Are any of the girls hurt?" asked Gina, one of the kinder teachers.

"No, luckily the girls are all fine, just shaken up."

Meanwhile, I delayed my classroom observations and Janet and I hurried to the kindergarten room to see if we needed to phone an ambulance, get ice, phone a family member or help in any other way.

After what seemed like three hours—but was actually about 20 minutes—everyone had calmed down and one of the mothers volunteered to drive Mrs. Jenkins to the emergency room at the hospital. Several hours later, after an examination and X-rays, it turned out she had broken the top of her humerus bone.

What started out as a fun outing for the Daisies turned out to be an unexpected experience. After the rest of the girls were picked up by family members, one of the mothers stayed back to chat with the teachers. She sheepishly confessed, "In hindsight, I don't think it was a good idea to get so close to the cows for a photo."

Science Night and the Garbage Bag Hug

"The Garbage Bag Hug! What a perfect name," said Marco. He was sitting on the floor inside a garbage bag with only his head sticking out. Harrison Barrett had the hose end of a vacuum cleaner sticking inside the garbage bag and was sucking the air out so pretty soon the bag was hugging Marco like a second skin. Harrison was a Robinson High School science teacher who was volunteering at the Baxter Elementary Science Fair.

"Can you feel that?" shouted Harrison. "Let me know if it's too tight. That's what external air pressure feels like."

"It feels weird, like something's pushing on my skin, like a really tight wet suit."

Marco Gleason was a fifth-grader at Baxter Elementary. He was a quiet, slim kid with shoulder-length black hair and was a frequent visitor to the principal's office. He had been at Baxter since kindergarten but this was the first time he had attended a school's evening function. Marco had several brothers and sisters so, with them to look after him and his parents both working at night, they had their hands full and never had time to bring Marco to things like this. His teacher, Lynn Vander, understood this and, as she had been trying to get Marco more interested in school, thought the Science Fair might engage him.

"Marco, I don't live far from where you live," she had said to him. "Do you think it would be okay with your parents if I came by and picked you up for the Science Fair? I'm picking up another student anyway, so it would be on my way to school."

Lynn didn't have plans to pick up anyone else, but if Marco could go she would find another male student to join them. She felt Marco would be uncomfortable if he was the only student riding in her car. So plans were made, and Lynn had brought Marco and Jeremy to school that evening. She was delighted to see how much he was enjoying the "Garbage Bag Hug" and the other events of the night.

This was the first year of the Science Fair at Baxter. It began as collaboration between Harrison and me. We had been planning for over a year and were thrilled with the results we were seeing. At least 400 students and parents packed the cafeteria. Harrison had his entire science department supervising activities and the room had been transformed for the event. There were science experiments in the middle of the room and along every wall. Stuffed paper reptiles, mammals and amphibians made by students hung from the ceiling. Laughter and chatter could be heard throughout the room.

Marco went from activity to activity enjoying the multitude of science experiments. All of a sudden he stopped. His eyes expanded as big as saucers when he saw the huge brown and tan checkered snake. The high school science teachers had brought their own collection of reptiles. One of the teachers, Joe Morris, saw Marco.

"Come on over. Do you want to pet or hold Willy? He won't bite. He's very docile and tame." Joe was holding a large gopher snake. He must have been at least five feet long.

Marco was hesitant. He had never seen a snake before in real life, only in books and on television. He slowly walked up to Joe but kept his distance. He just stared at the snake.

"Go ahead, touch his back. It's okay. He's friendly."

Marco gently ran his fingers along Willy's smooth, silky back. Willy didn't seem to notice. Marco stayed there for a long time watching how Joe let the snake move along his arms. As he watched he seemed to grow more comfortable petting the snake. Soon Marco was rubbing Willy's back and eventually he let the snake wrap itself around his arm.

"See how gentle Willy is? Wrapping himself around your arm is his way of figuring out who you are. Would you like to help put him back in his cage?"

Marco smiled and his eyes lit up. It was unusual to see him show emotion instead of acting blasé and cool. He helped lift the huge snake into the glass terrarium. Willy's tail end was hanging over the edge of the glass as Marco lifted it up and put it down into its temporary home.

I asked Marco if he was having a good time.

"I didn't know science could be so much fun," he announced excitedly, as he raced off to the next activity before the evening ended.

The Science Fair turned out to be a win-win partnership between the high school and the elementary school. The high school science teachers brought their passion about their subject to the elementary students and it was exciting to watch their enthusiasm as they showed the younger kids how science worked. From petting snakes to learning about air pressure, I saw students all around the room engaged in discovering science and experiencing "Garbage Bag Hugs."

 "A master tells you what he expects of you. A teacher, though, awakens your own expectations." *~Patricia Neal*

The Intervention Specialist

*P*am was always there when we needed her, and she was an imposing presence on campus. She was irreplaceable. Pam was tall, outgoing, and possessed an infectious laugh. She could roll her eyes at you with a look that said, "Really, you expect me to believe that?" And many a student was the recipient of that look.

After graduating from college with a double major in police science and psychology, Pam was hired at a correctional facility. Her experience there taught her that most of the inmates were not bad people; just people who made bad decisions they wished they could redo. After a couple of years she decided she wanted to work on the other end of the system, at the end where she might be able to impact student's lives and steer them in the right direction.

Pam made her decision at the right time. The Carson Student Center was implementing a new program in our school district in which a psychologist and an intervention specialist would be placed at some of the school sites, working with the staff to support students. Pam interviewed for the position of intervention specialist, was hired and placed at Baxter. That was the spring before I arrived as principal. In those first few months she became very familiar with many of the students and their families, so when she learned a new principal had been hired, she requested a meeting.

Pam was standing in the front office when I arrived one morning.

"Hi Jane," she said, as she extended her hand. "I'm Pam Olson and I work with the Carson Student Center."

"Hi Pam, nice to meet you. Come on into my office. Thanks for setting up this meeting. I've heard about Carson and I'm anxious to partner together."

What I thought would be at most a half hour meeting turned into two hours as I listened in disbelief to the stories Pam told me about several of the students at Baxter.

"I really had a connection with Charlie," she sighed. "But he would climb up onto the roof of the school. We had to remove him several times last spring."

"So what happened to Charlie?"

"We had to find a placement at a school that would meet his needs. Now he goes to a public school geared for students with emotional disturbances." Pam continued.

"His younger sister Lisa is still at Baxter and has her own anger control issues. Their Mom left the family when Lisa was four, and their father is a drug addict, trying his best to raise his children. "

"Oh my gosh! Is there any other family support for her?" I asked.

"Yes, there is an aunt who keeps a close eye on the kids and steps in when Dad is not available."

Then there was Monica; she was living with her single, alcoholic Mother. Monica was in first grade and was one of the reasons her former kindergarten teacher retired the previous June. She would kick and scream at the teacher. Last spring Pam had to spent part of each day in the kindergarten classroom, intervening when Monica threw her tantrums.

Carlos was a current fifth grader. His father and brothers were gang members and Carlos showed all the signs of following in their footsteps. According to Pam we needed to keep a close watch on him.

He would roam the playground, kicking other kids' balls out of their games and making fun of other students.

Pam continued pummeling me with stories of students we needed to offer support and structure to this year. That was why Pam was placed at Baxter. Discipline was one of our big issues, and we needed systems in place for students. I leaned back in my chair, looked at her, and let out a huge sigh.

"I'm sure glad you're here, Pam. I can't imagine trying to run this school without you. Being here to support the students and teachers is a full-time job. I don't think I could do that and be curriculum leader too."

Pam laughed. "For the most part, the kids are great. But a handful can take up most of your day. Don't worry, we'll work as a team."

~~~

Throughout the six years I was principal at Baxter, she and I did just that. We drove to homes together, met with students together, and laughed and cried together. The students and families loved Pam because they knew she cared deeply. She provided resources for the families when they needed clothing or shelter. Every year she organized a holiday drive where teachers and families would donate toys and she would personally deliver them to families who otherwise might not have holiday gifts. Pam made a significant impact creating a safe and secure environment at our school.

 "And time for reflection with colleagues is for me a lifesaver; it is not just a nice thing to do if you have time. It is the only way you can survive." ~*Margaret Wheatley*

Early Morning Attendance Visit

*J*anet brought the shiny red attendance folder into my office. My shoulders sagged in disappointment at what I read. Naomi Smith was truant again. So far, she had missed 23 of the first 30 days of school. Naomi was a third-grader, new to Baxter that year, and it was difficult to get her to stay in school.

"Naomi's still out? Have you heard anything from mom yet?" I asked. "Has she been sick again?"

"We don't know. We keep trying to contact her but she hasn't answered phone calls, E-mail or responded to snail mail. Her teacher's also been trying to contact her, but she doesn't answer his calls either."

~~~

Naomi's attendance concern prompted my visit to Wanda Curtis, Director of Student Services for the School District. Wanda was in charge of the School Attendance Review Board (SARB). She was a no-nonsense person and former principal of the district's continuation high school. She was tall, lanky, good-natured, and always enjoyed a hearty laugh, but when it came down to business Wanda was the one to get it done.

"Hi Jane! What brings you down here so early in the school year?"

I explained about Naomi's absences. After talking through the situation Wanda paused and looked at me. She had that look in her eyes, you know the one that says, *I've seen this before and I know just how to handle it.*

"Where does she live?"

"In Los Positos," I responded. Los Positos was a low-income housing project in Robinson and home to one third of our school population.

"OK," she replied, "meet me here at 7:00 tomorrow and we'll pay Mom an early morning visit. "

Usually when the school district visits first thing in the morning, it's for a 'bed check,' and unannounced to make sure the student is actually living in our attendance area. This visit was different. It would also be unannounced, but the purpose was to see what was going on in the home that was preventing Naomi from attending school.

~~~

Wanda and I met at her office early the next day and drove together to Naomi's home. We parked across the street from a cream colored duplex. On the dried-up front lawn stood one scraggly sycamore tree —otherwise the yard was void of vegetation. The shades were drawn giving the house an empty look.

"Do you think they still live here?" I asked.

"Maybe not—that often happens here in Los Positos. A family runs short on resources and they have to find another place to live. Sometimes they wait until they're evicted, leave hurriedly and don't think to tell the school."

I had been on this street many times before, driving students home or visiting families. This time felt different. I didn't know what to expect. I looked around to see if anyone was watching us.

We walked up to the front door and that was when I got a big shock . . . . BAM! BAM! BAM! Wanda banged on the front door. "THIS

IS THE ROBINSON UNIFIED SCHOOL DISTRICT. OPEN THE DOOR NOW! NAOMI NEEDS TO BE IN SCHOOL! WE NEED TO TALK ABOUT WHY SHE HASN'T BEEN AT SCHOOL! OPEN THE DOOR NOW!" BAM! BAM! BAM!

Holy cow! I thought. I was afraid the pounding and yelling would wake up the whole neighborhood. People peered out of their windows. I felt vulnerable standing there on that front porch. I wanted to crawl under a rock. I didn't know what was going to happen.

Finally, a voice from the other side of the door answered, "Okay, okay, you don't have to yell. I'm coming."

The door opened. The house was dark inside. There stood Naomi's mother, thin, sleepy-eyed, and wearing a faded yellow fleece bathrobe.

"Are you Naomi Smith's mother?" demanded Wanda.

"Yes, I am."

"I'm Wanda Curtis, Director of Student Services for the Robinson Unified School District, and I believe you know Jane Blomstrand, Principal of Baxter Elementary. Naomi has missed 23 out of the last 30 days of school. Why hasn't she been in school?"

We were invited inside and began a lengthy conversation with Naomi's mother providing every excuse imaginable for why Naomi was absent so many days. The core of the problem seemed to be that Mom was depressed, having trouble dealing with life, and just wasn't getting Naomi to the bus stop in time. She didn't have a car to drive her, so once Naomi missed the bus there was no way to get her to school, except to walk. As a result, Mom just had her stay home, which was convenient because she used Naomi to run errands and do chores for her. Both Wanda and I suspected substance abuse.

After talking through the situation, Wanda looked at Mom. "You know the State will withhold your SSI check if your child is not in school on a regular basis. I'll be contacting the Social Security office this afternoon if Naomi is not in school today. It's your responsibility to see that she gets to the bus stop on time and that means Monday through Friday. If you have difficulty with that, you need to contact Ms. Blomstrand or my office, and we will help find you support. In the meantime, we'll notify you of the meeting date with the SARB. They're very helpful and have many resources to help you. We look forward to seeing Naomi in school today."

As we walked back to the car, Wanda looked at me. She had a small, sly smile on her face, "That's how you have to do it; the first thing you have to do is get their attention."

Naomi came to school that day and missed only one day of school the rest of the year. In fact, a couple of months later, she entered a drawing in our school art contest about "What is Your Favorite Place." Naomi drew a picture of her school and teacher.

~~~

At the end of the year the SARB panel presented Naomi with a certificate for excellent attendance. Her smile when she achieved that award warmed my heart. Her mother was in the back of the room. I thought I saw a tear run down her cheek.

"Eighty percent of success is just showing up." ~*Woody Allen*

Pig Noises in First Grade!

When I saw him sitting in the office I wanted to hug him, he looked so scared. He was adorable with curly black hair and huge brown eyes. He stared up at me with the most forlorn look, just like my Labrador puppy did when he had chewed my favorite pillow. I had not seen Emile in my office before and was surprised to see him sitting there. First-graders were usually not sent to the principal unless their transgression was pretty serious, so I wondered what he had done to warrant this visit.

"Hello Emile, show me your paper and we'll talk about why you're here."

The paper was something students received when they were sent to the principal's office for a behavior issue. They were asked to write about why they were sent to the office, and what they could have done differently to avoid the visit. First graders were asked to draw pictures of their story. Emile showed me his paper.

"So tell me about this first picture Emile. What are you doing?"

He looked at me, bit his lower lip and hesitated. "I'm making pig noises."

"Oh, where were you when you were making pig noises?"

"On the carpet."

"What was your teacher doing?"

"She was talking to the class."

"So, you were making pig noises while Mrs. Larson was teaching the class?"

He nodded his head.

"Tell me about this next picture, the one showing what you were supposed to be doing while your teacher was talking?"

"It shows me sitting on the rug listening to Mrs. Larson."

During this conversation I found it difficult to keep a straight face. Emile's very somber conversation about making pig noises was so endearing and cute. To me this was a minor situation compared to what I usually dealt with in my office. However, to Emile, this was a very serious affair. He had been sent to the principal for making pig noises in the classroom while the teacher was teaching. I had to treat it seriously because what he had done was disrespectful, and he needed to learn that it wasn't appropriate behavior. So I held it together and kept my attitude thoughtful while talking with him.

"Emile, do you know why you come to school every day?"

He looked at me with those big brown eyes for a very long time, I could tell he was probably deciding how I wanted him to answer that question.

Finally he responded. "To learn?"

"Yes, that's right. Do you think you were learning while you were making pig noises?"

"No."

"What were the other students around you doing while you were making pig noises?"

"They were laughing at me."

"Do you think those students who were laughing at you were learning what your teacher was teaching?"

"No."

"So, by making pig noises you not only stopped learning for yourself, but also for those students who were laughing at you, because they weren't listening to your teacher, right?"

"Yes," he said, as his eyes flooded with tears.

"When your mother sends you to school what does she want to happen for you?"

He again hesitated for a while before answering. "To learn."

"Would your mother be happy about you making pig noises and not learning?"

"No."

By now big tears ran down his face.

I handed him a tissue.

"I'll tell you what, Emile. You agree to pay attention to Mrs. Larson when she is talking in the classroom and to take your learning seriously, and I'll agree to come visit your classroom, and when I see you listening to your teacher I'll make sure to let her know that I noticed how well you were paying attention and learning. Is that a deal?"

He nodded. I walked him out of my office and sent him back to class.

There was a part of me that questioned why this situation had been sent down to my office. It seemed it could have been taken care of in the classroom. But then I wasn't the teacher and I didn't know about everything else that had gone on that day so I didn't want to pass judgment. The teacher and I would have a conversation about Emile and the incident. In the meantime, hopefully, Emile learned that making pig noises while the teacher was talking was not appropriate.

 "The greatest compliment that was ever paid me was when one asked me what I thought, and attended to my answer." *~Henry David Thoreau*

It's Difficult to be Brave

One year ago, Lucas Jones, one of our 9-year-old students, was diagnosed with an inoperable brain tumor. His young body had gone through radiation and chemotherapy for several months with no success in shrinking the tumor. He had missed some school during his treatments, but on the days he was able to attend he was the Lucas that all the kids loved. Blond-haired, brown eyed, slimly built with an infectious smile, Lucas loved to tell jokes and make people laugh. His favorites were knock-knock jokes.

His other passions were Star Wars and Monopoly. He built many Star Wars creations out of Legos. On a visit to his home I saw them displayed in his bedroom on various shelves his dad had built.

"I can create cities on the shelves my dad built," Lucas told me. "See over here, I have a place for the Imperial Landing Craft and over there for the Millennium Falcon."

"Wow, where does Luke Skywalker live?" I asked.

"I'm just starting his shelf, here's his scout ship." He grabbed the model and pretended to fly it through the air. "He uses it for reconnaissance missions with the Rebel Alliance."

I was amazed at how much Lucas knew about Star Wars. That passion carried over to his love of Monopoly. He had a game called "

Lucasopoly," which he created himself. Instead of Boardwalk and Park Place he had names like Planet Batuu, and Jabba's Throne Room. Lucas loved his friends and his teacher, and being able to attend school had given some normalcy to his life.

We were a month into the new school year. Lucas's mom, Sandra Jones, contacted me on a Sunday to ask if she could come in to meet with us about Lucas in the classroom. The next morning his teacher, the school psychologist, the reading specialist, the district nurse, and I met with Sandra before school.

Sandra taught part time at the local intermediate school. She had continued teaching through this ordeal with Lucas as it helped provide a balance in her life. She walked into the meeting sharing hugs with everyone.

"Thank you all so much for being here on such short notice," she said. As difficult as this has been, our family is finally at peace with everything."

She was so stoic and strong the rest of us had to put on a brave front for her. Eye contact with Cindy Howard, our Reading Specialist, let me know how she felt.

"As you've probably noticed," Sandra stated. "It's increasingly difficult for Lucas to speak clearly, his eyes are crossing, and his walk is wobbly. We've seen a significant decline in the last few days. I wanted to ask if it's possible to have an aide assist him in the classroom? He desperately wants to be at school and around his friends, but I'm concerned about his safety. As long as he wants to come to school, I'd like to make that possible for him."

"Absolutely," I said. "We'll do whatever we can to make school a safe and welcoming place for Lucas. Will he be here today?"

"Yes, if that's okay, he'd like to be here. Should I let his Dad know to go ahead and bring him this morning?"

"Yes, I'm glad he'll be here."

I introduced her to Cindy and explained that she had agreed to be with Lucas in the classroom if necessary, until we found someone who could be with him as long as needed. We told her we had the perfect person in mind, one of our strong special education aides, and that I would let her know as soon as we had that solidified."

Tears formed in Sandra's eyes.

"Thank you for being so accommodating," she said. "He doesn't really want an aide. It's embarrassing for him. But I told him it was important for his safety and that she wouldn't sit next to him but just be there if he needed her. He accepts that idea. He just doesn't want to bring attention to the fact that he has difficulty walking without stumbling and he needs to hold on to furniture. He wants things to be as normal as possible."

Sandra also said that they were now working with Hospice, as the doctor had not expected Lucas to have much time left. We all had tears in our eyes but were trying to hold it together because of this beautiful, brave, unwavering woman who was trying to do whatever she could to make her son's life as happy and normal as possible. Her sole purpose was to be there for him, and that meant not falling apart. We needed to do the same.

I just could not imagine her situation. It was every parent's worst nightmare. I fought back my own tears as I asked if there was anything else we could do for her.

"There is one more thing," she said. "Because of his increasing physical limitations the other kids are beginning to notice and wonder what's happening to Lucas. They may be asking questions their parents don't know how to answer. May I write a letter to the parents in his class and could you send it out for me? I'd like to give them some words to use when talking to their kids about Lucas."

"That's a wonderful idea," I told her. "We can do that for you as soon as you're ready."

The meeting ended with lots of long hugs. Cindy stayed to talk with me.

"I hope I can do this," she said. "I want to because I want to support Lucas and his family. I just hope nothing happens when I'm with him."

"You'll be fine. Just use your instincts. Keep your distance when he seems okay, and get closer to him if you sense you're needed. I'll keep checking in on you throughout the day, and you have my cell number if you need me."

I sighed and gave her a big hug as she left. *Would I be able to do what she was going to do today?* I wondered.

The day went without a hitch. I relieved Cindy at lunchtime and stayed in the library with Lucas as he played board games with his friends.

"Hey Josh," I heard him say. "You were only supposed to move three spaces not five."

He was smiling his little crooked smile, obviously enjoying being with them. However, at one point I did notice that he had his head down on the table. Being at school was the right thing to do, but it did take its toll on him physically.

A few days later Lucas needed the wheelchair. He resisted at first, so we used it only for bathroom breaks. Soon the wheelchair became part of Lucas' new normal.

~~~

A week later, Rusty, our custodian, was in front of the school greeting students as they were being dropped off when the Jones' car drove up. Rusty quickly pulled the boy's wheelchair out of the trunk and rolled it up to the car door. As he opened the door he saw a frail little boy slumped over in the backseat. I thought I saw Rusty's eyes water.

"Good morning Lucas, great to see you," Rusty gently teased. "You ready for a Star Wars ride?"

Lucas glanced up. "Hi."

Rusty pushed the wheelchair closer as he unbuckled Lucas' seat belt, scooped him up and placed him it.

"Let's go, buddy. This Scout Ship is ready to roll?"

You could see a little crooked smile form on Lucas' face as Rusty wheeled him off to class.

That was Tuesday, Lucas' last day at school.

Two days later Sandra sent us an email that Lucas had passed away in her arms the night before, surrounded by his loving family.

That Friday Lucas' teacher and class held a small ceremony. They planted a tree outside the classroom to honor him. The teacher had purchased blue bandanas for each student to wear. Blue had been his favorite color. The students each wrote a letter to Lucas' family and they were placed in a large envelope to be delivered that afternoon. Some of the notes read:

"Lucas was a special friend to me, he was always smiling."

"Lucas and I used to play Star Wars together."

"Lucas always was nice to everyone, they will love him in Heaven."

"I loved Lucas but I know you loved him more."

Through this experience with Lucas and his family we learned about bravery, perseverance, compassion and love of life. These lessons were more impacting than any textbook could ever teach us.

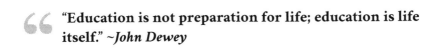

"Education is not preparation for life; education is life itself." *~John Dewey*

The Cupcake Committee

$\mathcal{I}$t became a very heated discussion in the faculty room! Both sides felt passionate about the subject for very different reasons. Each side had valid reasons for their beliefs. In one camp it was all about the *cognitive domain*, student academic learning and how we already didn't have enough time in the day to cover what we needed to teach. The other camp was all about the *affective domain* and the need to create a positive environment in the classroom where students felt accepted and safe. I had no idea that bringing up the subject of celebrating student birthdays in class would bring out such intense emotions.

I had broached the subject at our faculty meeting because the district was looking at how to maximize student-learning time. The Superintendent had asked all the principals if our students were getting the most out of their educational day, and were there procedures we could adjust or change that would add to our instructional time? I knew there would be strong feelings on both sides as we started our discussion about the wishes of the district. I brought up the subject of celebrating student birthdays with cupcakes at school. Gina was the first one to speak.

"You've got to be kidding," she said. "We already have so much emphasis placed on testing and grades. These kids have too much pressure put on them. This is one area that makes students feel special and good about themselves. We can't give that up."

"But do you realize how much time it takes away from instruction when you add it all up?" asked Wes, a Special Day Class teacher. "If you have 25 students in your class and it takes about 15 minutes for each celebration, which doesn't seem like much time, but 15 minutes times 25 students is 6 hours and 15 minutes. That's a whole day of instructional time lost."

Hands shot up all over the faculty room from teachers and support staff eager to speak. Sidebars of conversations took place at each table. Feelings were very strong on both sides as the discussion continued.

"Well if you think about instruction it's the perfect opportunity to teach the social skills of politeness," remarked Paula, a first grade teacher. "We need to enforce what is or should be taught at home. At the parties we teach the kids how to wait for their turn, how to say please and thank you—there are great lessons learned so instruction is going on."

"Yeah, but I don't see those skills in our state standards." Francie, a fourth grade teacher retorted. "We need to be teaching curriculum, you know: math, writing, reading, science, social studies—we don't have enough time to fit everything in as it is. I don't allow treats for birthdays in my class. We put a party hat on the kid's head, sing happy birthday and that's it. My kids are fine with that."

"Another thing we haven't mentioned is that in some religions they don't celebrate birthdays. What about those kids, we can't ask them to leave the room while the birthday celebration is going on, and you know how uncomfortable it is for them to sit there and not participate."

I just listened as the discussion continued. Good points were being brought up on both sides. I knew how I felt but I wasn't going to interject my opinion at this time.

"What about the parents? What will they think about not being able to bring in cupcakes on their kid's birthday? I don't think they will be very happy."

"Actually, some may be relieved. Some of our moms bake pretty elaborate cupcakes! I remember when Mrs. Farnsworth brought her cupcakes in on a cookie sheet, she confessed to me that she took them out of the Safeway box because she was too embarrassed for others to know she bought them at the grocery store."

"Well, maybe it's better for kids with allergies to have them come from the store rather than baked at home where there may be things like nuts and eggs used in the home kitchen."

Whew, I didn't anticipate this big of a discussion but good points continued to emerge. Where would we go from here?

We decided to form a committee to do some research, talk more to staff and talk with parents. Maybe check with other schools to see what they do. Teachers from both sides of the issue volunteered to participate. So that was the inception of "Cupcake Wars" with the Cupcake Committee.

The Cupcake Committee took its work very seriously and after many focus group meetings, surveys and one on one conversations they finally came to a conclusion that covered both the cognitive and affective domains and seemed to be a win for all. It was decided we would celebrate student birthdays with a birthday hat and a birthday song. It would take no more than one to two minutes and no food would be involved. Our birthday celebrants would have a memorable day and receive special attention on their birthday, but we wouldn't be losing an entire day of instruction eating cupcakes. An exception was made for kindergarten.

Through this exchange of teamwork and compromise we were confident we produced a wonderful balance between celebration and academics (or the cognitive and affective domains).

Uncovered

---

*A*nnie poked her head into my office. "Jane, do you have a minute. I have a problem with my classroom."

"Sure, come on in."

"It doesn't have anything to do with my kids. They're all great. But I keep finding stuff on the ramp in front of my portable."

"What kind of stuff?"

Our conversation continued. Annie Holmes taught first grade at Baxter and she shared with me that she'd been noticing things left on the ramp leading up to the door of her portable classroom for a couple of weeks.

"Sometimes I find kids clothing like hoodies, jackets, sweaters all lined up on the railing of the ramp."

"Really, like clothes from our lost and found?"

"Yeah, it's almost like someone is barricading the ramp." She was animated. "You know when you were a kid and used all the sheets and blankets in your house to make a fort, draping them all over the furniture? It's kind of like that." She paused. "I wonder if it's kids from the after school program playing hide and seek games."

She also explained she started noticing large pieces of cardboard, like appliance moving boxes that had been torn apart, left in piles on the ramp.

"I thought it must have been the after-school students again." she remarked. "I would throw it away but the cardboard kept reappearing, not every day, but periodically I would find them. I finally decided I needed to talk to the Director of the After School Program."

"Did that help?"

"Well I'm not sure. He said he would look into it and ask the students. He hadn't seen anything himself and said he usually keeps the kids so busy they wouldn't have time to play out by the portables. I haven't heard back from him yet."

"Okay, I'll follow up with him and see if he's discovered anything. But please let me know the next time you find clothing or cardboard or anything else on your ramp; I'd like to come and take a look at it myself. Do you need any other help with this? We can get Rusty to clean up or take stuff away if you need."

"Will do. Thanks. I've removed it all. I don't care if kids are playing there, it just would be nice if they picked up after themselves."

~~~

About a week later I heard from Annie again about this issue. I had arrived at school early when she rushed into my office.

"Oh Jane I'm so glad you're here. You won't believe this. Remember when I told you about the stuff on the ramp of my classroom? I think someone is sleeping there. I arrived early this morning because my students are performing in a play today and I wanted to get the classroom ready. As I approached the portable I saw the clothes again hanging on the railing but it looked different this time, there were more of them and they shielded almost the whole ramp and there was lots more cardboard too. As I got closer I saw what looked like a big lump under the cardboard but I could see feet sticking out. I just turned around and raced down here. I assume it's someone sleeping and not dead. What do I do?"

"Oh geez, let's go find Rusty. We need to have him with us before we go up there."

Rusty, our head custodian, was a big, body-builder type of guy, and if we were going to approach a homeless person I wanted to have support from someone like him. We explained the situation to him. The three of us headed out to Annie's portable near the edge of the playground. As we approached we could see multiple pieces of clothing hanging down providing a comfortable shelter. There were gray puffy jackets, small pink, white and yellow sweaters, green, black and red hoodies and enough other items of clothing to form a clothesline around the perimeter of the ramp.

Also, leaning on the outside of the back of the ramp was a rusty gray bicycle with multi-colored strings hanging off the handlebars and tan-colored stuffing poking out of the torn black leather seat. It looked like at one time it had belonged to a kid with its streaming colors hanging off the handgrips.

As we walked closer we could see the large pieces of cardboard covering the ramp were not laying down flat and definitely covering something rather large. We intentionally raised our voices as we approached.

"Rusty, what do you think this is here? Are these jackets left here by our students?"

"It sure looks like a lot of them, and look, there's a bicycle leaning up against the classroom."

That loud conversation prompted some of the cardboard to move and as it raised up a man poked his head out.

"What are you doing here?" Rusty declared, raising his voice. "You do know this is a classroom and students will be arriving soon."

"I'm sorry man. We'll get out of here right now."

When I heard him say "we" I glanced at Annie. She looked back at me wide-eyed and right then another head poked out of the cardboard. This one was female.

"You guys need to find another place to rest your heads at night. This is a school and you can't sleep here." Rusty retorted.

"I know, I know. We'll be outta here in a minute."

Luckily they were both dressed because immediately the two sleeping people began rushing around gathering their cardboard and other belongings.

"And leave those jackets here, I believe they belong to our kids."

The guy grabbed the cardboard and the woman commandeered the dusty gray bike down the gravel path that led to the portable classroom, and they were quickly on their way off the school grounds.

"Oh my gosh," whispered Annie. "Thank you so much for taking care of them. I don't know what I would have done. I couldn't believe when I saw that this morning but I had no idea there were two people sleeping there. I'm just glad it wasn't a dead person."

I turned to Annie. "Are you okay? Do you feel comfortable going into your classroom now?"

"Oh yeah, I've just got to get in there and set it up for the play this morning." And she rushed up her ramp.

I was happy it turned out to be as easy as it was to get the homeless couple off the ramp and out of school. I was pretty sure that we would never see them again. Rusty and I agreed he would check the classroom portable areas each morning as he arrived, and I went off to phone the superintendent and head of maintenance to apprise them of the situation.

These two people seemed harmless and would probably just find another place to spend their nights. It was sad that they had nowhere to go with a roof over their heads and were forced to sleep under cardboard on a school classroom ramp. But, I had a school to run and my main concern was for the safety and well being of the students on my campus. Our schools are open and available to the public, which can be very positive, but also very dangerous.

Let's Play Candyland!

*H*e bounded into the principal's office carrying a "Candyland" game . . . "Who do you want to be? I want to be King Candy. You can be Princess Frostina, Lolly or Peppermint whatever his name is..."

I smiled. "Oh, so it's Candyland today is it. Okay, I think I'm going to be Lolly because I would like to live in the land of lollipops."

~~~

In the last month Eddie and I had been playing one kind of game or another every time he got 6 out of 6 stickers on his behavior chart. We had played Dinosaur Bingo, Chutes and Ladders, Bug Bingo and sometimes we just read books. Eddie got to choose. That was his reward for respecting his teacher, not blurting out, and for acting appropriately when he didn't like something. Each hour of the day, when his behavior was on target, his teacher placed a sticker on the chart taped to his desk. At the end of the day he took his completed sticker chart home, and every morning a new one was taped to his desk. Each day that he received all 6 stickers he earned 15 minutes to collect his reward with the principal.

"I got all the stickers again."

"Wow, Eddie that is terrific. You must be very proud of yourself."

"Yeah . . . let's start. I'm King Candy and you're Lolly."

In the last 9 days he had earned 6 stickers 6 times and 5 stickers twice. That was incredible progress for a boy who formerly burst out emotionally when he didn't like something, had been suspended for biting and hitting, and had threatened girls with bringing a gun to school to kill them.

The sticker chart had been initiated since the last meeting with Eddie's mother. That meeting actually had been very disappointing. His mother attended, but not his father. *Why didn't his father attend? Didn't he get the severity of his son's behaviors?* The group had discussed Eddie's impulsive and inappropriate behaviors with his mother, stressing that she consult with his pediatrician about Eddie's lack of impulse control. She said she would do that the next time he had his annual check up. *You've got to be kidding,* I thought. *Why would you wait and not do it right after this meeting?* I spoke up.

"It's really important not to wait to discuss this matter. We don't know what's causing this kind of behavior but it's severely affecting his relationships with other students as well as his academics. Your pediatrician may offer advice on how to help Eddie control his impulses so he can be more successful at school. We highly suggest you try to meet with him as soon as possible."

As the meeting continued we discussed many things, including how Eddie's 13-year-old brother called him 'stupid' and put him down frequently. Perhaps that's why Eddie called himself stupid so often.

"Have you tried talking to his brother about how calling Eddie stupid affects him?"

"He doesn't listen to me. Eddie is so hyperactive he always disrupts Ethan's things and that makes him mad. So he calls him many names—stupid is the milder one."

"I would also talk to your pediatrician about this when you meet with him.

It was apparent that his mother was frustrated but didn't know what to do. She had three boys, the older one was out of control and now she had to deal with Eddie. We had decided to try the sticker chart as a way to provide an incentive for Eddie to adopt more positive behaviors.

The chart seemed to be working. Eddie loved the extra attention he received. Now it was fun to come to the principal's office. No more comments from him about how we were ruining his life. It wasn't an easy ride toward improving Eddie's behavior. There certainly were ruts in the road, but we seemed to be moving forward on a smoother path. For now, Eddie was happier, his teacher was happier, and Mom liked receiving those emails that said "Eddie had a good day today!"

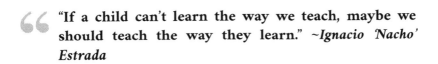

"If a child can't learn the way we teach, maybe we should teach the way they learn." ~*Ignacio 'Nacho' Estrada*

THE FIFTH INNING

HOW I STARTED IN THIS JOB!

An Unusual Hiring

*W*e had made a lot of progress as a team since I was hired as principal of Baxter Elementary several years ago. As I reflected on the past few years I recalled the incidents surrounding my hiring and my first couple of weeks on the job.

~~~

My husband and had I boarded a flight to Wisconsin on the afternoon of my interview at the Robinson School District. We had arranged to meet my brother and sister-in-law who had travelled there in their motor home--we would stay with them while visiting the Osh Kosh Airshow.

As I relaxed in my seat I had thought about my morning interview. I had prepped myself for questions I expected to be asked, so I felt comfortable with my answers. Having been on several previous interviews, I did have an idea of the kinds of information that would be asked; something about discipline, teacher evaluations, parent communication, curriculum; pretty much standard areas in education. But what was odd was how relaxed I had felt. Perhaps it was because my main focus that week had been on preparing for our vacation.

What I had really agonized over was what to wear for the interview. How trivial that seemed now, but experts always say that first impressions occur in less than fifteen seconds. Everyone in that interview room would form a judgment quickly, so I wanted to make a positive impact.

In my administration program at the university, we were told never to wear red to an interview because it was too dominating. My traditional interview suit had been navy blue with navy blue heels. I always added a subtle scarf to provide color. But, for some reason, maybe because I was feeling good about this upcoming interview in Robinson, something told me to go ahead and brave it. I chose to wear a reddish/pink suit and a multi-colored, floral silk scarf.

When I arrived at the district office, I remembered immediately having a good feeling about the place. The people I saw in the halls were smiling and chatting with one another. The woman in the Human Resources (HR) office welcomed me, asking if I was there for the interview and when I told her who I was she immediately went to get Wayne Russell, the Assistant Superintendent of HR.

After a few minutes, a tall, good-looking man with glasses perched on top of his head and a big smile came out. With his tie loosened and his shirtsleeves rolled up, he had that slightly rugged look of an administrator who used to be a P.E. coach.

"Hi Jane, I'm Wayne Russell, nice to meet you! Thanks for being willing to interview on such short notice. We know you're leaving on vacation this afternoon so we appreciate your squeezing this into your day."

"Thank you for rescheduling the interview before I leave, I appreciate that."

"We're looking forward to talking with you about our principal position. The interview room is right down the hall, so let's go and meet the team."

When we entered the room I hesitated. Fourteen people sat around a very long boardroom table, all looking at me--that was intimidating! My heart started beating faster but I managed to maintain my composure. Most interview teams have about six or seven people at the most, making it easy to connect with each person when answering questions. This would be very different, how does one make a personal connection with fourteen people in forty-five minutes?

Wayne directed me to the head of the table where I sat down. He introduced me to the team, explained the process, offered me a glass of water, and the questioning started. They went around the room with each person asking a question. As I answered I began to realize that my background as a Literacy Specialist, my work with English Learners, and the collaborating I had done for years with parents and teachers seemed to be exactly what they were looking for. My shoulders started to relax as I saw many affirmative nods around the table.

The interview concluded with lots of smiles and thank-yous. I left my contact information with Wayne.

I felt good about the interview. Maybe it was a good thing I'd had the trip to focus on; it may have taken away some of the normal interview jitters. Or maybe Robinson was the school where I was meant to begin my new career as a principal.

The next evening we were halfway across the country in Wisconsin. It was a balmy evening at the Osh Kosh Air Show. We had watched the amazing parachute and aerobatic teams strut their stuff. We delighted in the skydiving, the drone show, the latest innovations in the world of flight and many examples of the history of flying. We were exhausted after our first day and my brother had just poured an appreciated glass of Pinot Noir when I received a call on my cell phone. I stepped away from the group to answer.

"Hello." It was difficult to hear because of the roar of airplanes overhead.

"Is this Jane?"

"Yes, it is."

"This is Don Stanton, Superintendent of Robinson Unified School District. You interviewed for a principal position in our district yesterday. I always like to do a second interview with our finalists.

Would you be able to come into my office on Monday to meet with me?"

I just about dropped the phone. Had I heard him correctly? After all these months of interviewing I was finally being considered for a principal position and here I was half way across the country!

"Thank you," I responded, "I'm delighted to be considered but I did mention to HR that after the interview I'd be leaving on vacation. I'm currently in Wisconsin," I paused a moment to let that settle and then continued, "I'm really very interested in this position. Is there anything we can complete on the phone?"

He hesitated for a moment. "Well not yet. Are you fine with me contacting your current superintendent?"

"Certainly. I've advised him I had an interview with Robinson."

"OK, then let me make that call and I'll get back to you Monday evening. In the meantime enjoy the air show."

I hung up the phone. My heart was pounding. I'm sure I had a huge grin on my face. The others were looking at me with questioning expressions.

"Who was that?" my husband asked.

"You won't believe this. That was the superintendent in Robinson. He asked if I could come in to meet with him on Monday for a final interview."

"That deserves a toast," announced my brother. He poured a second glass of wine for all.

"Wait! Wait! Not so fast. Let's not put the cart before the horse. I'm a little superstitious. If he calls back Monday evening and offers me the position, then let's have a toast. In the meantime, keep your fingers crossed."

~~~

The call did come in on Monday night and I was offered the position. Of course I accepted. "Now we can have that toast," I told my brother.

Two weeks of vacation remained before returning home. My head was spinning with thoughts and plans and emotions. I was really going to become an elementary school principal!

I wanted to focus on the rest of our trip but too much was going on in my head. The first thing I needed to do was to call my current principal and superintendent. They knew I was interviewing but needed to know I had accepted the job.

Next, I purchased a letter-sized pad of paper and as we continued on our way to visit friends in Toronto I recorded my thoughts. What is Baxter Elementary like? What are the students like? What will I do to get to know my new staff and the school? Should I set a meeting with each separately? How will I introduce myself to the students? What kind of parent support does the school have? Ideas swirled. It felt good to get them out of my head and onto paper where I wouldn't forget them.

For the next two weeks my husband drove while I talked and wrote. I hadn't realized how much I had been thinking and planning for this new chapter in my life.

" **Turn your window into a Mirror.** " ~*Anthony Mohammad*

The Robinson School District

I had read a little about Robinson School District before the interview at their district office, but now that I would be their principal, I studied up on the district.

Robinson was in the same county where I lived, but further east, nestled against a beautiful inland estuary. Over 75 percent of the students qualified for free and reduced lunch and there was a rich mixture of ethnic diversity, the exact demographics I was looking for. I wanted the richness of a mixed community and Robinson offered that environment in a much smaller setting than the larger urban school districts nearby. With a population of about 53,000 people it was a diverse community in a suburban setting. A perfect combination!

Being over the hill from where I lived made it seem almost as if it were in a different state.

What I remember most when I began my job was driving over that hill at sunrise when the rays of light were glistening off the water just ahead of me.

I quickly learned about the deep sense of pride the residents of Robinson felt for their community. I remember a comment Janet, made one day. "Why do so many people who live where you live think we are low class?"

That surprised me but I knew what she meant. People who lived in Robinson were aware of the perception many outsiders carried about their city because of its higher crime rate and lower economic status but this was their community, they knew the richness it possessed, and they resented other people making judgments without first getting to know them.

Who were these residents? They came from many different walks of life. The Italians' family roots went way back to when the town was a fishing village. Their ancestors fished along those same shores where the blazing morning sun still dances off the water.

The Latino roots went far back to the time when the Los Mariscos Rancho was granted by the Mexican government. This tract of land, with its rolling yellow sand dunes extending to the sea, was laid out as the site for the city. There are still Quinceañeras every year celebrating Latinas coming of age.

When coal was discovered in the local hills, the Ruby Hills Mine commenced operation. Steel mills popped up in the community. The town was named Ruby Hill, soon to be changed to Robinson. Many African Americans came from the South to work the steel mills, and their music and deep sense of togetherness resonate to this day.

Towards the end of World War II many Filipino military personnel were recruited by the U. S. Army and came through Robinson's Camp Spencer. They also brought with them a strong pride in their heritage and homeland.

Whether attending a school board meeting, a city council meeting or the famous Community Festival, I would soon come to find that the blending of all these rich cultures working and living together is what makes Robinson the special community it is today.

First Day on the Job

$\mathcal{J}$ was nervous that first time I walked through the front doors of the Robinson District Office to meet Don Stanton, the Superintendent. We were to have an orientation to the district and to my new job as principal of Baxter Elementary. It seemed like a long journey, a year and a half in the administrative leadership program, several job interviews, and then Robinson willing to take a gamble on a fresh face with no principal experience.

I was looking forward to meeting the superintendent and learning more about the school and district where I would be working so I was surprised when the Assistant Superintendent of HR greeted me. "Hi Jane, Don had to go to Sacramento this morning so he asked if I'd meet you and give you the keys to Baxter so you can get started. He'll meet you tomorrow morning and give you his orientation."

He handed me a set of keys and asked if I had any questions before I went to the school. I was crushed. This was not what I expected. I had been looking forward to meeting the superintendent. I felt like a kid who arrived at a birthday party and discovered there was no cake and ice cream. But I thanked him, took the keys, and said I didn't have any questions at that time. I was sure I would soon have many. I left the district office and headed for Baxter.

As I entered the school office a very attractive woman with long, dark brown hair and stunning brown eyes greeted me. She was sitting behind her desk.

"You must be Jane."

Not, 'Welcome to Baxter' or 'I've been looking forward to meeting you,' or getting up to shake my hard or extend me a warm greeting. Just "You must be Jane." That was Janet Warren, all business. My first impression was that Janet could probably freeze the sun with her presence. That would change later as we got to know each other and developed a wonderful working relationship. I quickly learned that she was one of the most efficient office managers in the district. After chatting with her briefly I walked into my new office.

I took a deep breath and let it out slowly, pausing a moment as the realization came over me. Before I went on vacation two weeks ago, I was an experienced literacy specialist in a high-income school district. Now I was an inexperienced principal of a school where over seventy-five percent of the students qualified for free and reduced lunch. This would be one of the biggest challenges of my career, and this room would be my office, where I would do my work, my new second home.

I glanced around. The walls were bare, painted off-white. In the far corner was a tan L-shaped desk—one side had a credenza with two shelves stacked on the back. It was positioned under a window; more precisely, the shelves were blocking the window. The only items on top of the desk were a black stapler, a scotch tape dispenser, a telephone, and a black plastic two-tier tray that contained a manila folder with two documents inside. A gray metal file cabinet sat next to the desk. Inside the drawers of the cabinet were papers, neatly filed in dark green Pendaflex folders that held information about everything from asbestos to yard duty.

On the opposite wall was a second door which opened onto the foyer of the school. Along this wall was an empty two-drawer bookshelf, and in the middle of the room, a round table with four chairs. These matched both the desk and bookshelf: tan, wooden and bland.

That was it. No welcoming posters with inspirational sayings about education, no visible binders containing budgets, School Site Plans, test results, or school information. The former principal had left earlier in the year, and an interim principal had been in place since that time. Neither had left under positive circumstances, so I would have little or no contact with them. Basically, if I wanted to know anything about the school I would need to start looking through those Pendaflex folders, and I would certainly need to get on the good side of Janet.

My mind transitioned back to the manila folder in the black tray on the desk; I opened it to look at the papers inside and picked up the top one. This document was a memo from the interim principal about a student who had been transferred to another school and should not be let back into Baxter under any circumstances. The description of his behavior caused me to wince. Apparently he bullied other kids, walked out of class whenever he wanted to and actually hit a teacher on the arm when she took something away from him. I was glad to know about him. The other document was the Individualized Education Plan (IEP) for a second grade student describing his behavior modification plan. This plan was to address behavior such as running on the roof of the school during the school day. Wow!

As I sat at the desk I began to feel overwhelmed. I looked around my new office. It was cold and unwelcoming. What had I gotten myself into? I felt uncertain and actually, at that moment, pretty unsure that I was the right person for the job.

I was looking down when I heard footsteps. A young man walked into my office.

"Hi. You must be Jane, our new principal? I'm Barry Arnold. I teach third grade here."

"Hi Barry, pleased to meet you. It's my first day, actually my first hour, at Baxter. I'm just checking out my new office and starting to get acquainted with the school. How long have you been teaching here?"

"I've been here two years. Just long enough to get to know our cast of characters. The majority are really good kids, but you're gonna have your hands full with some of them. The last principal didn't like to discipline, so students got used to pretty much making up their own rules."

I told him about the notes in the manila folder.

"Oh yeah, Charlie. We did have to get him off the roof a couple of times. I can give you a heads-up on some of the other regulars you'll most likely see in your office."

I took careful notes as Barry filled me in on some of the students at the school. It sounded as if we had a few wannabe gang members on campus. I knew my first principalship would be difficult, but this looked like my endurance would be tested.

After Barry left I decided to walk through the campus. The interior hallways were tile from floor to ceiling. It was nice, clean-looking and light blue. The only problem was that there were several places where chunks of tile had fallen off the walls and not been replaced. A big four square foot patch was missing from the feature wall in the main lobby. All that made the school look a bit like a war zone.

I found my way out to the playground, after making a mental note that I had better have Janet give me a map of the school, because I wasn't sure I knew how to find my way back to the office. The playground didn't look much better than the hallways. Instead of a nice, shiny, colored metal play structure with a couple of slides and interesting things to climb on and crawl through, there was a gray swing set with four swings, one of which was broken.

What I saw of Baxter in that short morning was very different from what I had been used to in my former school. It didn't seem right. All students deserve to attend a school where it looks to them as though someone cares. There was a lot of work to be done.

~~~

That evening at dinner as I was telling my husband about my day and what I saw at my new school, I was surprised when a tear rolled down my cheek.

"What's the matter? Aren't you happy about your new job?"

"I am, but I'm not sure I can do it. I don't know if I have the right experience."

"Well," he said, "you'd better let them know tomorrow, because if you're not gonna stay they'll need to find someone else quickly."

"Oh, I don't want to quit. All I really want is just to feel sure I can do it."

From across the table he squeezed my hand. "Of course you can do it, this is what you've been preparing to do. They're lucky to have you."

---

*"It's not so much that we're afraid of change or so in love
   with the old ways,
But it's that place in between that we fear.
It's like being in between trapezes.
It's Linus when his blanket is in the dryer. There's nothing
   to hold onto."* ~**Marilyn Ferguson**

Maintenance Issue

*A*fter a good night's sleep and a therapy session with my husband, I had shaken off the apprehension of the previous day. He helped me remember why I had decided to become a principal, and that it was reasonable to expect a new challenge. I was ready now and with the shock of the situation over, I looked forward to getting started.

The superintendent, Don Stanton, was coming out later in the morning to meet with me and, as I anxiously awaited his visit, I decided to take a more thorough walk around the school to familiarize myself with the whole site. It was disappointing to see the poor condition of the grounds and buildings. It looked as if no one had cared about them for a long time. The playground was good sized but sparsely equipped. In addition to the centuries-old play structure, there were a couple of basketball hoops with torn netting - and that was it in terms of play equipment for students.

At the main entrance weeds encroached on the concrete path leading to the front door. The black paint on the handrails was chipped. The lawn was mowed but brown. Baxter Elementary looked drab and institutional. How would I feel about my own kids attending this school?

But what really jumped out at me again were the interior tile halls. It was disappointing to think students were soon expected to start school in a facility that looked so run down - as if no one cared

I hadn't expected that one of my first duties, as a principal would be getting the facility looking decent for the start of school. I had been prepared and excited to begin dealing with curriculum and instruction, and here I was thinking about how to fix missing tile in the halls. As I sat in my office, processing all this, someone entered the doorway.

"Hi, are you Jane? I'm Tim Esposito, Superintendent of Maintenance. I wanted to stop by to let you know my department is here to support maintenance needs at your school."

I looked at him for what may have seemed like a long time. My mind was connecting what he had just said with what I had just seen in the halls. How fortuitous that he had arrived right now!

"Hi Tim, nice to meet you. Thanks for coming by. You actually came at a perfect time. I just finished walking through the school, and I do have a question for you. Can we go out into the hallway?"

We walked into the lobby. I showed him where the tile had fallen off. "I noticed this in many places. Is this on your fixit list before school starts?

"No, sorry, we tried to glue that tile back many times. Just won't stick. Moisture behind the walls I'm told. School's due to be modernized when the next bond passes. Then we'll replace all this"

I looked at him, dumbfounded. I wasn't quite sure what to say. I wanted to tell him to go to Home Depot, buy another type of adhesive, and find one that would work. Being married to a builder gave me some knowledge about construction. I don't know how to build but I've learned enough to know you keep trying until it's fixed. It frustrated me that the guy in charge of getting stuff repaired would dismiss this and leave it as it was.

We parted ways. I hadn't wanted to get on the bad side of the person in charge of maintenance on my second day on the job, so I didn't say anymore then, but I wasn't going to let that conversation die.

Later that morning, when I finally met with Don Stanton, I found an opportunity to mention the wall tile issue to him. After talking for a while about some district concerns he wanted me to be aware of, I brought it up.

"Don, can we go out and walk through the halls for a minute? I want to show you a maintenance issue I noticed yesterday."

We walked through the halls together. I showed him every place the tile had fallen off. I shared my concerns about wanting the school to look welcoming to students. He didn't say anything; he just looked and ran his hand along the wall in several places. Don was a big guy, a man of few words and I supposed he intimidated a lot of people because he was not afraid to share his opinion. After a few minutes he stopped, pulled out his cell phone, and called Tim to come over to the school.

When he arrived, Don showed him the large area of missing tile in the front lobby. He asked him what had happened and why the tile hadn't been put back on the walls. Tim gave Don the same explanation he gave me. Don looked at him for a moment, ran his hand along the wall again, and turned back to Tim.

"Get this subbed out and have the missing tile replaced throughout the halls before school starts."

Then he turned and looked at me. "Jane, can we go back in your office for a minute? "

My heart fluttered, I felt like the kid who was summoned to the principal's office. Did he think I was wrong to have brought this up and he just didn't want to say anything in front of Tim? Should I have waited and not made waves so soon? I wasn't sure what to think.

Inside my office he was brief.

"Thanks, Jane, for bringing this up," he said. "I want to make sure Baxter gets off to a good start this year."

"Thank you for being willing to take care of it so quickly." I told him. "I really appreciate the support."

"Well, it should have been taken care of a long time ago. Please let me know if there is anything else I can help you with."

Whew! I breathed a sigh of relief. He understood my concerns as leader of the school, didn't question them, and took steps to support what needed to be done. Hooray! It felt so good to have that kind of support come from the superintendent because I was sure this was not the last time I would be asking Don to come to my aid.

Devastation

I was in in my new principal position for three months when I opened the local newspaper one Sunday morning and was stunned with this news.

A 15-year-old Robinson High School student, Stephanie Martinez, had attended her friend's Quinceañera rehearsal in a neighboring city. She was frustrated with her friends teasing her as she was trying to learn a difficult dance step. Abruptly she left the rehearsal at midnight and walked by herself down a dark stretch of highway in Robinson, presumably toward her home four miles away. Stephanie never made it home. Everyone at the party thought someone else had given her a ride home, but when her mother awoke at 3:00 a.m. to find her daughter missing, she phoned the police. That day bloodhounds led police to a deserted area along that dark stretch of highway and found her garment bag. Inside were her black patent-leather shoes. A huge effort was launched to try and find her. Eight days later Stephanie's asphyxiated body was found face down near a landscaping business along that same road. The path she walked down was only a half-mile from my school.

An innocent young girl upset and not knowing how to appropriately handle her embarrassment and frustration, now not getting the chance to grow and learn from her mistake. What a tragedy! It devastated the small close-knit community and rocked the surrounding cities.

Many of us at Baxter had developed a habit of stayed late finishing work or came to school on Saturdays when it was quiet. Now we all were fearful and afraid of doing that. When I accepted the principal job several of my friends had asked me "Why are you going to work out there?" The crime statistics in Robinson were much higher than the community I had been previously working in. I chose to work in that area because of its diverse student population. I thought I had stepped into my dream job now I began to wonder if they were right.

On Monday morning I met with Andrea Ogden, our school psychologist to brainstorm how to handle the devastating situation with students and staff.

"Oh my God Andrea. I can't believe this happened. It's a parent's worst nightmare."

"I know. It is so tragic," replied Andrea. "Do we have any students who were related to her or were close friends or neighbors of her family?"

"I had Janet check and it doesn't seem so, her home was not in our school boundary even though she was found in our area. I was worried about how upset our students would be but it seems most of them don't know about it. Several of the 4th and 5th graders have made comments so their teachers are talking to them on an as needed basis."

"Probably best to handle it that way with the students. You know I'm available if any students need to talk. What about the staff? How are they holding up?"

"That's what I wanted to talk with you about. We have a staff meeting this afternoon and I'd like to discuss safety procedures we could all follow. I don't want to alarm folks but we should address the issue."

"Right. What did you have in mind?"

"Well, for starters I don't think anyone should come in to school on a Saturday by themselves. I can put out a notice if I am planning to be here and then people can let me know if they want to be here too. Also, parking cars together and as close up to the front door as possible is a good precaution."

"Good ideas. We should mention locking doors if you're here after hours, and not propping outside doors open to make it easier to get back inside."

We talked together for the next hour coming up with some other ideas about community building for the staff meeting that afternoon. We felt it was important to talk about the situation as a school community, make a plan and let staff know we were there to support them.

The staff meeting went well and everyone acknowledged our new safety procedures. Our night custodian was female and she carried a walkie-talkie to communicate with custodians at the other schools if she saw anything suspicious. I continued to work late on many nights out of necessity but would always let her know when I was staying late. We would pull our cars up on the expansive walkway leading up to the front doors of the school so they were close when we left school for the night.

People were beginning to relax when our world was rocked even more. Within two months, three other young women and one young man, all between the ages of 24 and 32, were killed in Robinson. Now it appeared to the police that this was the work of a serial killer and set off panic among the residents that this person might be loose in their midst. It was constantly on the minds of our parents who were all very concerned. It was a frequent topic brought up in conversation when students weren't around. People were on edge, constantly aware of their surroundings and suspicious of anything different. There was a lot of chatter amongst the high school staff. The high school counselors were busy supporting students who felt afraid. Student life at Baxter went on as usual, our students were younger and generally not aware of the grizzly events that had occurred in their community.

Fear dissipated as time went on and soon, with the reduction in newspaper coverage, people resumed their normal lives. What was sad to me was that there was a vast amount of newspaper coverage of Stephanie's death and the details surrounding her murder, but that was not the case with these others. Some of the other victims had a history of prostitution and it was almost as if their lives didn't have as much significance.

There were suspects investigated over the years, but none were charged with the crimes. To this day the murders remain unsolved. The Robinson Police Department keeps trying to reignite interest in the case hoping someone might remember something leading to an arrest and conviction.

THE SIXTH INNING

THERE ARE SOME DAYS THAT YOU JUST WOULDN'T BELIEVE!

The Classroom Box

I remember the morning vividly when I opened the newspaper and read: *"Students Put in Box in Classroom."* The headlines jarred me and a chill ran down my spine as I read my school's name in the article--Baxter Elementary.

Frantically I scanned the piece. A former special education teacher at Baxter, had lodged a complaint with the Disability Rights Education and Defense Fund. She notified the local newspaper that the school was putting students in a closet when they acted out. *That's absurd; it's not a closet. It's where kids like Timmy can go when they become so frustrated they want to scream, hit others, and throw everything in sight.* I immediately called my superintendent to see if he knew about the article.

The "closet" was in our new Counseling Enriched Class (CEC) class. It was a 6-foot square room enclosed on three sides with padded material, like furniture moving pads, on the walls. The fourth side was open with no door. A classroom aide would sit at the opening, supervising closely, assuring the safety of the student inside. Students could either go into the room voluntarily or at the request of a teacher.

I threw the paper down on my desk, frustrated that they would print an article like that without interviewing anyone at the school first. Then I left my office to go talk with the classroom teacher, Wes.

153

"Did you see the front page of the newspaper?" I asked with an exasperated tone.

"You've got to be kidding, you know who that is don't you?" he responded.

"No, I don't. Should I?"

"Oh that's right. Tamara Jessup was a special-education teacher here before you came."

"Of all people she should understand what this class is all about. Why would she report something like this to the newspaper?"

"There were some issues and the district released her. She was very disgruntled and I'm guessing she wanted to get back at the district. She still has friends here but she doesn't like me very well, we had some philosophical issues disagreements."

We agreed we needed to talk with Percy Jorgenson, our District's Director of Special Education about contacting the newspaper.

~~~

Later that day I learned Percy had contacted the newspaper and a reporter would arrive after school to talk with us. Percy planned to be there, along with the teacher and a couple of parents and students in the class. Timothy Pratt would be one of the students at the meeting. Last year, Timmy attended Alternative World, a non-public school for students with severe emotional disabilities. He had just returned to Baxter to be in our new CEC.

I remembered him telling me, "I am so happy to be back here at Baxter for fourth grade with my friends. I'm gonna try to be really good and control my temper so I can stay here." Timmy was the kind of student the class was designed to support.

At the end of the day we met with the reporter. We all sat together around a typical school table in the small classroom. She spent the next hour and a half interviewing the teacher, parents, and students

As they were talking, I glanced over at Timmy, remembering what it had been like for him two years ago.

In second grade he would explode when he couldn't understand something. He would shove his desk, throw books, and become so disruptive he had to be removed from the classroom. I recalled counseling him in my office on what seemed like a daily basis.

After many failed behavior plans and in-depth meetings with Timmy's parents and specialists it had been decided by all to transfer him to Alternative World to provide a different learning environment.

That climate had been successful for him and it was decided he was the perfect candidate for our new CEC. With this program of support Timmy was a different student this year. Being able to meet individually with a counselor once a week, and regularly with a small counseling group, helped him learn how to deal with frustrations in a more positive manner and he was having a very successful fourth grade year.

During the interview the reporter asked Wes what helped make this class successful. "One key component is that we have regular counseling for the students," responded Wes. "Each student gets one-on-one and small group counseling every week. We also have a positive behavior management structure in place where the kids earn rewards for doing what's right, and then we have a 'time-out' room for releasing frustrations in a controlled setting, what you referred to as the "Box," he said facetiously. "The goal of this class structure is to help students develop necessary tools to handle their frustrations so they can focus on learning."

"And I would like to add," I told her, "another key ingredient is a strong, compassionate teacher who cares and has high expectations for his students."

The reporter took notes and asked a lot of questions. We concluded the meeting and when she left I felt she had a good understanding of our new CEC program.

At the end of the day, I reflected on the interview. When the reporter had asked Timmy how he felt about being in the "box" in his classroom Timmy's response was "If we didn't have that room for me to go into when I need a time-out I wouldn't be able to be back at this school with my friends." The reporter paused to look at Timmy. "Thank you Timmy," she said. "That helps me understand." She closed her notebook and walked out of the classroom.

~~~

She never wrote a follow-up article explaining the benefits of the CEC. It was frustrating that she never retracted her prior reporting and that I should be the one responsible to ask for, or demand, a follow up article. I probably should have asked her to come back, observe the class, and write another more positive article but I had a school to run, so we just continued our jobs doing what we thought was best for educating students.

 "A good teacher must be able to put himself in the place of those who find learning hard." *~Eliphas Levi, French Occultist*

A Tough Decision

*M*rs. Conrad was anxiously waiting in the office to speak with me about her son, Bradley. She was a lovely woman with a kind face and a soft-spoken manner.

She fiddled with her car keys as we sat down to talk. "It's about my son, Bradley. He's in Mr. Parker's fifth grade class and is the youngest boy there. My husband and I would like to have him spend another year in fifth, rather than move him on to middle school next year. We think he's immature and not ready for sixth grade."

"Tell me about your son, and why you think it's in his best interests to repeat a year."

Her story revealed Bradley's past six years in elementary school. His birthday was November 28, four days before what was the cut-off date for kindergarten entrance. Many of his peers' parents had their children spend another year in pre-school because their birthdays were later in the year.

When Mrs. Conrad and her husband had asked his pre-school teacher if he should stay another year at her school she said he was smart and got along well with other children, so he would probably do fine moving forward. She also said if the teacher had concerns, she would let them know and he could spend a second year in kindergarten.

So Bradley started school as a four-year-old who would turn five in three months. He had a slow start, but by the end of the year he caught up with the other students and the kindergarten teacher told the Conrads that their son was a little on the young side but would do fine in first grade.

But now a number of kids in his grade were at least a year older, and no one was younger than Bradley.

She continued her story. "In first and second grade it was the same. Bradley got off to a slow start each year, and by the end of the year he had caught up with his classmates. I remember in second grade his teacher had a poster on the wall with a big tooth on it. Every time a student lost a tooth their picture would go up on the poster, and they would get to wear a crown for the day. Bradley never earned the right to wear the crown." Mrs. Conrad's eyes welled up with tears.

I brought out the Kleenex.

She hesitated before continuing. "In the fall of third grade, Bradley's teacher told us he was immature for his grade. She said he had friends and was keeping up with the class academically, but he would get upset easily when he didn't understand something, and he would lose his homework frequently and not turn it in. He was pretty disorganized."

The Conrads decided this could be the time for Bradley to have a bonus year so they scheduled a conference with his principal to discuss the situation.

"She listened to our story," said Ms. Conrad. "Then she asked us a lot of questions about Bradley, like was he happy at school? Did he have friends? But then after our conversation she said the school would not retain Bradley."

"Did she say why?" I asked.

"Yes, she showed us his test scores and told us he was doing well academically, therefore she couldn't justify a reason to hold him back.

She said the district was not in favor of retaining students; research showed it didn't work."

Oh my gosh, I thought as Mrs. Conrad was talking, my heart went out to her. I understood her story on a personal level and I got a lump in my throat listening to her. She could have been talking about my son, Jackson.

Thirty-five years ago my husband and I had been through this very same story. Our son had been very young for his grade. We had asked every teacher from pre-school through second grade and they all said the same thing; he's too bright; he will get bored if he repeats a grade. Jackson came to us at the end of second grade and told us he wanted to be in second grade again next year and when we asked him why he told us two things: everyone else's teeth had fallen out but his, and all the boys that ran faster than he did in the relay races were a year older. In his seven-year-old mind he put all this together and decided he didn't belong in the same grade with these kids. We talked to his teacher and the principal, and both of them advised against keeping him back so we didn't.

I looked at Mrs. Conrad; we both had tears in our eyes.

"You just related the story of my son," I told her. "I went through this same experience thirty-five years ago."

Her shoulders relaxed as she sat back in her chair. She looked at me apprehensively. "How did it turn out for your son?"

I told her we ended up having Jackson spend another year in fifth grade before he went to middle school, just like they were thinking of doing for Bradley.

"It became apparent at the end of fourth grade that the demands of school were catching up with Jackson. He began to lose assignments and not turn them in. He didn't like it when he had to leave class for something like band or speech and felt like he was missing something. School began to lose its appeal for him and became more like a chore. In fifth grade he stopped wanting to read for pleasure. When I asked his fifth grade teacher how he felt Jackson would do in middle school he said, "Oh, don't worry. He'll do Okay." Okay didn't seem right for a

159

kid as bright as Jackson. We knew we had to talk with him and make a decision. Once he started middle school, there would be no turning back."

"Did he end up staying in fifth grade?"

"Yes."

"How was Jackson with that decision?" Mrs. Conrad inquired.

"We approached him with the idea. We talked about the ups and downs of what it could mean for him. We gave him time to think about it because we weren't going to make that decision if he was not on board. After much thought and a little apprehension about not going on with his friends he felt he would be able to handle it and make new friends. It wasn't like he didn't know any of the kids in the grade behind him; he had played sports with them for years. So, in the end, he agreed with it. "

"So, how was Jackson's experience in middle and high school?" she wanted to know.

"He enjoyed both, had a positive experience and now is a very happy and successful adult. In fact, Jackson and I had a conversation about this a couple of weeks ago. I asked him as he looked back on that decision whether it had affected him in any negative way. His answer was "No, it was fine. I think it was definitely the right decision for me."

"So it can work and be successful!" Mrs. Conrad said with a sigh of relief. "We have looked at private schools, schools in neighboring districts and even thought of home-schooling. We had not thought of keeping him in the same school. Thank you very much for taking the time to talk to me. I feel so much better just knowing that you understand how we feel about this decision and that it could work."

She was sitting up straighter in her chair now and appeared stronger and more confident than when she walked into my office.

"Then I definitely don't want him go on to middle school next year," her voice was firm. "I have a meeting with the school psychologist next week to talk about the decision. I just hope she doesn't tell me all the psychological damage I could do to my son by having him repeat a grade."

"Don't worry, she 's a good listener; she'll hear what you have to say. I'll talk with her before your meeting and tell her about our conversation. She'll be involved as we talk about the best situation for Bradley next year."

Mrs. Conrad shook my hand and thanked me again for taking the time to talk with her. I knew the district feeling about retention. I, too, had read the research and the negative effects it could have on a student. I also knew that when it was done for the right reasons— developmental readiness—it usually was very successful. Bradley was the perfect candidate; it just would have been easier if the decision had been made in kindergarten or first grade. I vowed I would do everything in my power to help Mrs. Conrad follow her heart, because I agreed she was doing what she thought was right for her son.

~~~

Three years later I saw Mrs. Conrad in downtown Robinson. She came up and hugged me.

"Bradley has had a very successful two years in middle school. Thank you so much for helping us make the right decision for him."

It was reassuring to hear this. Thankfully, with California's new entrance requirement for kindergarten, kids like Bradley and Jackson will never again start their formal school careers as four-year-olds.

False Alarm Embarrassment

*T*he morning was relatively quiet. After reading the hundred plus new emails that morning I was on my way to visit classrooms. As I walked through the office I stopped to give Janet a message when all of a sudden the fire alarm started blaring.

"Are we having a fire drill? I asked surprised. "I didn't have it on my calendar."

"No," Janet responded, alarmed. "We didn't have one scheduled. I don't know why that's going off."

"Well, I assume it's real. I need to grab my walkie-talkie to contact Rusty and see where this came from and who pulled the alarm. You check the faculty room and work room," I said to Janet. "Make sure everyone there exits of the building." I rushed back to my office.

As I was heading out the door Rusty rushed in the office and to the fire alarm panel. He disconnected the alarm. We looked at him confused.

"False alarm, a kid in the multi use room pulled the switch."

"You've got to be kidding. The whole school will be out on the blacktop. I can see the teachers taking their classes out now. Do we know who the kid was who pulled it?"

"Nope, the parents club is in there setting up for the Art Show during Open House tonight and they panicked when they heard it. Luckily I was nearby. One of the moms ran out and saw me and yelled to me that it was a false alarm."

We all looked at each other in frustration.

"Well, let's treat it just like a practice and consider this our monthly fire drill."

"Shall I give the all call to go back to class now, Janet asked?"

"Yep."

Rusty and I walked outside to where the teachers were lined up with their classrooms and we heard Janet's voice over the outdoor speakers.

"The fire drill is over, thank you all for such a quick and efficient exit. You can return to your classrooms now."

"Oh my gosh!" I exclaimed. "I just remembered, the fire department. We need to call them and tell them it was a false alarm."

As we rushed inside to make the call we could hear sirens along the main road out front. We all looked at each other. "Too late."

Rusty raced out front to intercept them.

~~~

With the false alarm behind us and students and teachers safely back in their classrooms we turned out attention to the cause of the pulled fire alarm lever.

"I'm going down to the multi use room and talk to the parents in there and see if I can find out what happened."

As I was walking out the door one of the mothers hurriedly rushed into the office. She looked panicked as she glanced over at me with a look that said *I wish you weren't in here right now.*

"I'm Heather Peters and I'm so sorry, it was my two-year-old son who pulled the fire alarm. I'm totally mortified. I was holding him and standing near the alarm box with my back to the wall. He just reached over and pulled the lever down. I'm so embarrassed. Can I pay for anything? I feel like I should reimburse the fire department or the school or something, I heard the sirens."

Rusty, Janet and I looked at each other and started laughing.

"Don't worry about it, Heather. We just figured we've had our practice fire drill for the month. Now we don't have to conduct the one scheduled for next week or have an extensive investigation about this one."

She looked so devastated I walked over and gave her a hug.

"It wasn't your fault, or your son's. If that's the worst thing he ever does, you're lucky."

"Thank you, that makes me feel better but I am still completely humiliated. Now can I tell you the worst of it? After he did that and it caused such a reaction from everyone in the room, he reached over to do it again. He thought it was fun. Can you believe that?"

We had a good chuckle together over the incident. Luckily no one was hurt; it only disrupted a little classroom instruction. This was nothing compared to a couple of years earlier when we had a fifth-grader pull the alarm thinking it would be funny. That caused a huge investigation.

Heather left with her son, and I went back to my office to contact the superintendent. I also contacted the fire department; I felt they would also get a chuckle out of the incident.

A few minutes later Janet came into my office with a smile on her face.

"Heather just brought her son, Joshua, in to apologize. He was so cute. His mom was holding him and he buried his face in her shoulder and finally in a little soft voice said, 'I'm sowwy I did that.'"

We talked about how kids aren't born knowing what's right and wrong. That's our job, as the adults, to teach them, and this was a good learning experience for Joshua.

Non-Re-elects Are Never Easy

*L*ast fall, two weeks before school started, one of my fourth grade teachers, Penny, walked into my office. She looked miserable and, from her expression, I predicted this wasn't going to be a conversation I should look forward to.

"Jane, I'm so sorry to be coming to you with this news right before school starts, but my husband was just offered a new job, and we are moving out of state in a week."

My heart sank! This is a situation all principals dread, having to hire a teacher at the last minute. Teachers had been assigned to their classes, and students had been placed in the right class for their needs. Now, Eduardo, who was strategically placed in Penny's class because of his high performance, would be placed in an unknown situation. Hiring a teacher right before school starts is like putting your hand in the grab bag and pulling out a number.

~~~

That afternoon, I had sequestered myself in the district HR office, looking through teaching applications, when I spotted Rob Hamilton walking in the door. He was neatly dressed in a dark blue suit and paisley tie, looking like someone who was there for a job interview. Rob was in his late fifties, friendly, outgoing, and a lot of fun to be around. He had been a pastor at a local church for about twenty-five years, and related well to both adults and kids. I met him through his wife when they would volunteer at Baxter family nights. She was an office manager in our school district and was always very helpful to me as a new principal.

"Hi Rob, what're you doing here all dressed up?"

"I just turned in my application for a teaching position. After all these years working in the church, I decided to try teaching. I applied to an intern program, but to be accepted I need a full-time teaching position. I was hoping there might be an opening here in Robinson."

Was I dreaming? I had to pinch myself to make sure I was awake. From what I knew about Rob, he seemed to possess all the skills necessary to become a good teacher. I'd learned to trust my instincts in selecting effective staff. He might not know curriculum yet, but we could teach him. In addition, he had all that counseling experience as a pastor. Our fourth grade teaching team was very strong and would be good support for him.

"What a coincidence, Rob. I just learned one of my teachers is moving, so I'm looking for a fourth-grade teacher."

Well, I ended up hiring Rob and thought I had snagged a match made in Heaven. Fast-forward nine months. Now here I was sitting in my office across from Rob, having to let him know I was not going to recommend the district rehire him next year. What had gone wrong? I had pulled the wrong number out of the grab bag.

It was one of the most difficult decisions a principal has to make. I agonized over it for weeks, often losing sleep at night. I consulted with associates and weighed the pros and cons many times. I worried whether I should give him more of a chance; there was always the possibility he would improve. He did relate well to the students and they liked him.

There had been two difficult situations involving students in his class that made me relieved Rob was their teacher. Raymond had a brother who was killed in a drive-by shooting. It was Rob who wept with Raymond and his family and helped them heal. And when Jaquan learned that he had been diagnosed with leukemia, it was Rob who counseled him and his family, helping them deal with the illness. These students and families had been lucky to have Rob's support.

On the other hand he had terrible classroom management, disorganized lesson plans, and refused to accept support from his peers. But we tried, believing we could help him with these concerns. After all, this was just his first year. He was an intern taking classes, and he hadn't completed student teaching.

I even provided a stipend to one of the fourth grade teachers to mentor Rob but it wasn't long before my hopes for him faded further. His university supervisor called to tell me Rob had not completed his courses nor turned in his end-of-semester project. She also said the university was ready to drop him from the intern program. With a heartfelt appeal and his charming demeanor, Rob had been able to convince her he had just been in over his head with his new job. He vowed to complete everything and get back on target so she agreed to give him one more chance and extended his deadline.

But, that sent off an alarm in my head.

About the same time, Francie Vincent, the fourth-grade teacher that I was paying to mentor Rob, came to me with her concerns. "Jane, I have a problem with Rob. You asked me to meet with him every week for support, but he always has an excuse why he can't get together. We've only met once since school started. He just blows me off. I really don't think he wants the support."

"Hmmm! Maybe I didn't make it clear to him. Having this support was not an option; it was a requirement as an intern teacher. I'll remind him. I won't tell him you came to me, I'll just ask him how it's going."

"Also, all of us fourth grade teachers have offered to help him, knowing he's just an intern. We told him we'd give him lesson plans and classroom management tips, but he doesn't seem to want help from any of us."

These conversations concerned me. I began frequenting Rob's classroom more often. Rarely did I see a lesson plan, and when I did, there was little evidence of meeting standards. In fact, I didn't see much actual 'teaching.' Rob consistently had students read a chapter in the textbook and answer questions in writing about what they read, but I never observed any discussion about the content. There was virtually no teaching going on.

We met after school to talk about my observations.

"Rob, I'm happy to see how well you relate to your students. I can see they enjoy being in your class. But I need to see lesson plans for what you're teaching, and they need to include specific standard-based objectives. I see a lot of assigning pages and having students answer questions in writing, but that isn't teaching."

"Oh I know, I'm sorry. I've been so swamped with work in my program. It's hard to find the time to write out lesson plans. Actually, I think I do better when I teach in the moment. But I'll work on that and make sure to write them out for you."

"The purpose is not to write them out for me. The purpose is to have organized lessons that focus on student learning. Also, Francie has agreed to coach and support you. Are you meeting with her once a week?"

"Actually, Francie and I have had a hard time finding a mutual time to meet. She's very busy, but I'll pin her down and we'll get some times set up soon."

Well, that was kind of like expecting a fish to walk on land. Changes didn't happen. Rob's lesson planning didn't improve, and he didn't take advantage of the support offered by his colleagues and mentor. His actions made my decision easier, but I still hated being in this situation. I was frustrated with Rob for not putting more of an effort into his teaching, and I was disappointed in myself. I had always taken pride in being a good judge of character and able to spot potential in a teaching candidate but I had missed the boat with Rob. Most of all I felt I had let down the students in his class. They deserved more.

I began to realize this was more than just being a new teacher with no experience. It seemed more about passive resistance and him just wanting to do things his own way. We had worked hard to build a collaborative community at Baxter; teachers worked closely together and learned from one another. It became obvious Rob wasn't interested in being part of a team. He didn't collaborate with his peers, he didn't take advantage of his mentor, and he wasn't following my suggestions. I thought about the students. Was having Rob as a teacher good for them? Would I want my child or grandchild in Rob's class? The answer was a resounding NO. I knew I had no choice. I had to release him.

Wayne, our Assistant Superintendent of HR gave me support and directives.

"Jane, you can release a teacher without specifying cause in the first two years."

"Well what do you say? Isn't that awkward?"

"Yes, it is but it's better not to get into a verbal discussion because at this point the decision should be solid and there's no need to justify it. Just be direct and to the point." He went on. "Just say it's not working out and you are recommending the district not rehire him."

So I made an appointment with Rob for Friday afternoon. I questioned myself. *What was the best way to handle this? How would I say this to him? Was I really making the right decision? Had I tried to support him enough? He was such a nice guy what would the other teachers think? His wife worked in the district office what would she think? Would he understand?* I agonized over how to handle this situation.

~~~

Friday came, and an encounter with Rob that morning confirmed my decision. I walked outside of the cafeteria to throw something away, and there was Rob behind the building, smoking. He knew smoking wasn't allowed on school grounds. I told him he needed to go out onto the sidewalk to smoke and he did. But then at 10:15 a.m.

recess, I walked out behind the cafeteria again, and sure enough there was Rob smoking.

That made my meeting with him easier. I knew I was right. He was a nice guy but he marched to the tune of his own drummer. Baxter didn't need a maverick on staff. Teaching is a delicate dance between teacher, student, and curriculum. It takes choreography and practice to flow smoothly. Rob was stumbling and not willing to learn the routine.

Our meeting that afternoon was short and to the point.

"Rob, I really like you and value your strengths as a person, but as a teacher here at Baxter it hasn't been what we were looking for so I am recommending the district not rehire you."

Rob was shocked. "I don't understand. What did I do wrong? I'll change whatever it is. I'll do whatever you want me to do!"

"I'm sorry it hasn't worked out but the decision has been made." I told him. "It just wasn't a good fit for you at Baxter."

I watched him as he left the office then I sat down and rested my head on the back of my desk chair. I had mixed feelings. On one hand, it was done. I had dreaded that conversation, and now it seemed as if an elephant had been lifted off my shoulders. On the other hand I felt incomplete, like I should have said or done more. But really, there wasn't more to do or say.

Rob finished the year professionally. I respected him for that. I never saw him again after he left Baxter. I often saw his wife in the district office, but she always looked the other way when she saw me.

More justification for my decision came during the summer, when our state test results were released. Eduardo, one of the most gifted math students I ever worked with, got a 70 percent in math proficiency. The only way he would receive lower than 95 percent was if he had not been presented with, or taught, the material.

Others can't always understand why personnel decisions are made and because they're confidential I couldn't share the background of the decision with anyone. But I knew the choice I made had been the right one for our students, and that was my job.

 "To please everybody is impossible; were I to undertake it, I should probably please nobody." ~*George Washington*

PTA Embezzlement

$\mathcal{I}$ was at home on a Sunday afternoon when I received a phone call that caused me to raise my eyebrows in surprise. Our State PTA representative, Patty Josephson called.

"Jane, I just finished auditing the PTA books and I found several withdrawals that show up on the bank statements but not on the books."

"Oh, really. What does that mean?"

"I don't know yet. The withdrawals total $3,000, and each is between $100 and $300. They were withdrawn over a yearlong period."

"What are they for?"

"I can't tell. I think you should contact the bank and ask them for the records."

She asked me to look into the details but not contact the PTA treasurer about them yet. I was surprised at that comment. This must be serious.

~~~

Baxter's PTA treasurer, Rosie Farnsworth, was the mother of three boys at our school. She was very involved in the PTA and volunteered weekly at the school. She was bubbly, friendly and always willing to help out at a moment's notice. We had immediately bonded over the fact that she graduated from the high school in my hometown. Surely there was an explanation for these withdrawals, but I felt I had better follow Patty's advice and look into the details before I asked Rosie about it.

The next day I called the bank to ask for copies of all statements and checks cashed during the past year. I pored through them one by one. My heart sank. What I found alarmed and disappointed me. Nineteen different checks had been cashed over the counter at four different branches of the bank. All had been made out to cash and signed by Rosie. Why? This didn't make sense to me. Why would someone who was so involved in the school on a personal level do this? Was she having financial difficulties? Did she think it wouldn't be noticed? Actually as I thought about it, she had delayed giving us the six-month treasurer's report. Knowing her, I hadn't suspected anything like this––just thought with three boys under the age of ten she was a busy mom.

As I investigated further I noticed that the PTA account had a two-signature requirement to cash a check. I was puzzled at how these checks could have been cashed with one signature. I went back to the bank to check it out. My conversation with the bank service representative was very surprising.

"I was reviewing our account for the Baxter Elementary PTA, and I noticed that we have a series of checks cashed with only one signature. There's a bank requirement on this account that there be two signatures. How could these checks have been honored?"

"That's not a bank requirement, ma'am, it's only a requirement of your organization to have two signatures on a check."

"Well, if it's a requirement of our organization on an account at your bank, don't you make sure all checks have two signatures?"

"No, ma'am, we don't have time to do that. If we tried to verify all the checks our customers cash, we wouldn't get our other work done."

"So what's the use of having that requirement if no one here follows through?

"That's something you should be doing before submitting a check."

"But what's to prevent a person from embezzling from an organization's account?"

"I guess nothing."

I was getting nowhere, so I asked to speak to the branch manager. He was not the same one I had worked with when we first opened the account. Darn, I thought, I knew the former manager would have helped me solve this. I introduced myself and explained the situation. "As you can see from our bank balance, this $3,000 is one third of the money we have raised for our school, so it is a big loss. I am hoping that the bank will be able to work with us to restore those funds for the students."

"I'm sorry ma'am, there was no negligence on the part of the bank in this situation and so we are not responsible to reinstate that money. I know what a disappointment this is for you and I feel very badly for the school."

"This is completely unfair for the students and Baxter. We thought we had a community partnership with the bank, and we trusted you to take care of our funds. I am very disappointed you can't resolve this for us."

As I walked out of the bank I could feel my frustration building. The manager's attitude infuriated me. He just brushed it off as if it was nothing. Three thousand dollars is probably a drop in the bucket to the bank, but to our school it was a big deal. I felt there was also a moral obligation involved. We had a relationship with the bank and they needed to try to work together with us. He had not seen the last of me. I was determined that the students weren't going to lose the money that had been raised for the school. I contacted Patty and explained the steps I had taken so far. We met together to strategize about what to do next.

"I still think we need to contact Rosie and ask her about all these withdrawals." I stated.

"This really is a police matter," said Patty. "We need to let them handle the situation, you don't want to get into the middle of it. Believe me I've seen this situation in more than one school."

I was so relieved we had Patty to help us through this situation. Going to the police seemed extreme but Patty knew what she was doing. This was the main reason I had encouraged our parents to go with the PTA instead of just a parent's club when setting up our parent's group. Now we had the larger PTA organization supporting us.

"Okay, I'm following your lead," I told her. But I was concerned. What about Rosie's three boys at school? What would this do to their family? I agonized over the idea of contacting the police, but this was a serious matter. This was embezzlement! It was a police matter.

We did end up contacting the police. Patty and I met with the detective together. He took all the information and copies of the cashed checks. He said they would do an investigation and get back to us.

In the meantime we still had our money at the bank to deal with. We could contact our local newspaper reporter, which would make a terrific headline story, but if we did that the name of the PTA treasurer would come out and that would be embarrassing for her boys. If we could we wanted to prevent them from knowing about this.

So I decided to write a letter to the bank's area representative, with a copy to the branch manager and the State PTA. I also copied our school district superintendent, who was aware of the situation. In the letter I explained the school's financial situation, the fact that many of our families were good customers at the bank, and that this kind of publicity could be negative for them. I was hoping this might make them change their mind.

It certainly did. Within two weeks we received a letter from the bank letting us know they were very sorry this had happened, and because they had a good partnership with our school district, they were going to restore the $3,000 to our PTA account. I smiled to myself and breathed a sigh of relief. Our main goal had been to restore the funds to the school and students. That was now accomplished.

That same week, late one afternoon, I received a phone call from the police detective.

"Hi, Mrs. Blomstrand, we have interviewed Mrs. Farnsworth and are ready to proceed with the case. How soon can you come down to the station to sign the paperwork?"

"I actually can come now if that works for you, but what paperwork will I be signing?" I asked.

"Let's go over that when you get here. We can talk through the whole case."

When I arrived at the station we sat down. He asked if we wanted to press charges.

"Actually, I'm very concerned about her family, she has three boys at our school and I'm worried about what this will do to them. The bank has restored our funds and that was my main goal in this situation."

"I understand completely. Would you rather not press charges at this time?"

"Yes, if that's okay."

He was sympathetic, and we agreed that we would not press charges at this time. Our goal had been achieved. The funds had been returned to the school. We would let the police know if there were any more incidents in the future.

The next day our PTA President came into my office.

"Jane, Rosie Farnsworth just turned in her letter of resignation as our PTA Treasurer. She said she has pressing family obligations that don't allow her to continue."

"Well, there are times when family has to come first. Do you have someone in mind to replace her? I asked.

I knew the State PTA was taking care of straightening out our books so there was no need to say anything about the situation. We found a new PTA treasurer and for the rest of the year Rosie and I politely existed in the halls together at school events. She would always look the other way when she saw me. We never spoke of the situation. I had wanted to talk with her, but Patty had advised me not to in case there needed to be a police investigation. It always felt very unresolved. I wanted to hear Rosie's side of the story. Why did she do it? I was saddened to think she had been that desperate.

~~~

Three years later, I received a summons to appear in superior court. The defendant was Rosie Farnsworth. That case was settled before it ever went to trial, so I never knew what the charges were against Rosie—but I had my suspicions.

The Strike

$\mathcal{A}$s I reflected on my day, I realized I had weathered one of the most intense situations I had ever experienced as a principal. After two years of collaborating with my staff to build a team, the district and the teacher's union had been unsuccessful in reaching a contract agreement. A strike had been called, and today was the first day. Teachers walked up and down the sidewalk, waving picket signs outside the school. Watching it was gut wrenching. Would this erode everything we had built together?

Confirming substitutes until ten o'clock the night before was not what I had envisioned when I signed on the dotted line. I was on the phone with one of the other principals making sure I had everything in place for school to start tomorrow.

"Pat, do you have all your substitutes lined up for tomorrow?"

"Yeah finally, the last one confirmed 15 minutes ago," she responded. "How about you?"

"I 'm not sure. I still have to hear back from one. But trying to get all the lesson plans for each grade level and get them placed in each classroom has been exhausting."

"I know, are all your instructional assistants and office staff coming in to work tomorrow. I hear some of them are honoring the strike and calling in sick."

"Oh geez, I haven't heard that yet. That would be a disaster for our special education classes." Some of those kids need their aids to function at school. My stomach churned as I thought of what the next few days might bring. At 11 o'clock I finally put what I could in place for the next day and fatigued I left to drive home.

When I arrived at school the next morning I almost had to redistribute the students once again as one of the substitutes, who had confirmed at ten o'clock the night before, didn't show up until just as school was about to start.

When he finally appeared, he greeted me with a huge smile and an outstretched hand. "Hi, I'm Michael Strong; just let me know where you need me."

I needed you an hour ago, I thought, as I shook his hand and thanked him for coming to help out.

Michael Strong was about 6 foot 4 inches and looked like an NFL linebacker. He wore multiple shiny gold chains around his neck and gold lame tennis shoes. He reminded me of Mr. T. from the A-Team on TV. He had never taught school, but was currently unemployed, wanted a job and was qualified to be a substitute because he had a Bachelors degree and had passed the CBEST test. I had been excited to have a young male to help out in the upper grades, but when he didn't arrive until the last minute I was unhappy and concerned about his ability to manage the classroom.

But here we were and would do our best. I had arrived at school at six that morning, giving myself ample time to prepare for the huge array of expected substitutes. While I had two teachers who made the choice not to strike, we still needed to fill 33 teaching positions. Signing on were retired teachers, part-time substitutes like Michael, and people who had never taught school. Even Anna, our Assistant Superintendent, had agreed to substitute for the day. It had been a long time since Anna had dealt with classroom management and she would probably find it stressful.

My first task, after securing enough subs, had been to prepare materials for them: lesson plans, class lists, rules and procedures of the school, basics in classroom management, and anything else needed for teaching students. So in the morning when they had all arrived we went over these materials first thing.

"What do I do if a student won't do what I ask them? Do I send them out in the hallway? Do I call you down here?"

"Do we take roll in the morning or at the end of the day?"

"Where do the students eat lunch?

When answering their questions I realized that some of these folks had never taught in a classroom. After clarifying procedures and policies I dismissed them to go to their assigned classrooms. In half an hour we were to assemble back in the multi-use room to meet students when school started.

Anna came to my office to check in. "Well Jane, I'm ready but I have to say, a little nervous. It's been a long time since I was in charge of a classroom."

"You'll do fine. You care and you like kids, so they're in good hands. We have a diverse collection of people subbing, and none familiar with our school, so it'll be interesting. Let's go greet the students."

It was chaos in the multi-use room as we all met to start the day. Brimming with excitement and anxiety the students squirmed in their seats awaiting final instructions. They didn't know what to expect or who their teachers were going to be, and substitutes didn't know the students they would be teaching. There hadn't been enough substitutes to cover every classroom so it was a good thing some parents had elected to keep their kids home. I was bleary-eyed from creating an endless number of class lists depending on which students and substitutes might show up. The whole thing had been a logistical nightmare and in constant change this morning. But we finally had all the students placed in classrooms, and everyone knew where to go.

~~~

At the end of our first day I thought about what had happened. It actually went relatively smoothly. Very few discipline issues showed up in the office, which was good. As I glanced out my office window I saw Michael and watched him as he exited the building. He walked out the front door of the lobby, stood in front of the school smiling, and eyeballing the teachers on the picket line. He paused there for quite a long time. I wondered what was going through his mind. Finally, he sauntered towards his car, slipped his hulking frame into the front seat and drove out of the parking lot, waving to the teachers as he went by.

Anna walked into my office as I watched him.

"What a character!"

"Yes, he sure is! I really liked him and how he connected with the kids. But I hope he shows up on time tomorrow. By the way, how was your day?"

"It actually turned out fine. A couple of boys decided to test the waters, but I remembered some tricks from my teaching days and we worked things out. If you need me, I can come back tomorrow."

I looked at her and sighed. "Oh thanks so much I can use all the moral support available. Dealing with the logistics is hard but it's just a matter of doing it. Dealing with the emotional piece is a different story. Watching Amy, one of our teachers who chose not to strike, walk out of school at the end of the day having to face her colleagues on the picket line and hearing their comments was sad. How will it be for her when the strike is over and she goes back to teaching across the hall from them?"

"I know, it's the people part that's hard. Let me know how I can help."

I thanked her and went back to scheduling subs, and planning lessons, class lists and procedures for the next day.

I was still in my office as it approached eleven p.m. I was exhausted. As I wrapped up my work and turned around for one last look at my computer I noticed an email from one of our striking kindergarten teachers.

"Jane, tell me about Mr. T, the guy with all the gold chains and lame tennis shoes. What's *his* story?"

Her message brought a smile to my face for the first time that day. Her comments reassured me that my concerns about losing the connection we had worked so hard as a staff to build might not materialize after all.

 "Our greatest glory is not never falling, but in rising every time we fall." ~*Confucius*

Different Perspectives

*T*here are times when you just need to sit back, listen and try to understand what someone else has to say even if you may not share the same perspective. We each craft our viewpoints depending on culture and background experiences.

That was the case when Leroy Simmons requested a meeting. He wanted to talk about an incident from the day before involving his third grade daughter, Renee.

At lunch recess some of her friends brought Renee into the office with a good-sized rope burn on her neck. The office staff treated it with ice and called home to alert Renee's mother to what happened. Mom talked with her daughter who said she was fine and wanted to stay in school for the rest of the day. Art Swanson, our vice-principal met with the students involved to investigate the incident and he wrote up the following report:

Renee and some of her friends had been playing jump rope on the yard at recess when a few third grade boys walked by. According to the girls, the boys grabbed their jump rope and began laughing and running away with it. Rather than request support from a yard duty supervisor the girls started chasing after the boys, creating more excitement. In all the chaos one of the boys, Robert, took the rope and tried to lasso Renee with it. He threw it around her waist. As she struggled to free herself from the rope it slipped up and landed around her neck. She fell down and the rope pulled across her neck causing the injury. The boys were given a consequence and would sit on the bench at the next recess. All students were all sent back to their classrooms.

I read through the report before meeting with Mr. Simmons, and was in the office when he arrived with another gentleman.

"Hello Mr. Simmons, I'm Jane Blomstrand, the principal. How are you today?"

"I'm fine, but I'm very concerned about the incident on the playground yesterday. May we go into your office to talk?"

"Of course, come on in." I ushered the two gentlemen into my office and motioned to the chairs at the table. All the while in my head I was wondering who this other man was; we had not yet been introduced to each other. He looked very business-like wearing a three-piece suit, glasses and carrying a briefcase.

We all sat down at the small table in my office. Mr. Simmons began. "I'd like to introduce Perry Granada, he is my attorney and works with many cases involving the NAACP. He is with me because of the gravity of the incident yesterday. "

That comment alerted me. NAACP, what's this all about? The incident involving his daughter was a benign playground occurrence; it was investigated and dealt with properly. I made sure to talk again with our vice-principal before this meeting to get my facts straight.

He continued. "You know what happened on the playground yesterday that caused the rope burn on my daughter's neck right? And I'm sure you are familiar with the history of lynching in my culture in this country."

He stopped and both men looked at me. Thoughts were flashing through my head at the speed of light. *I was shocked they were associating this incident with lynching? Did I need to have someone else in the room with me? Was he going to sue the district? Had we handled the incident correctly? Did we miss something? Should I stop this conversation and ask him to meet with me and our Director of Student Services at the district office?* I wasn't sure what to say. But I had to think fast. I decided to hear him out and then decide if I needed to involve the D.O.

"Yes I am. It's a terrible stain on our country's history. But, surely, you're not suggesting that the playground incident had anything to do with lynching."

"Well, actually when you have two White boys throwing a rope around the neck of a Black girl, I don't know what else you would call it."

"According to the vice-principal who investigated the incident one of the boys threw the rope around her waist, which in no way was acceptable, and when she ran to get away from it the rope slipped up around her neck."

"That is not the story that I was told, and my daughter has the evidence on her neck that suggests otherwise. Have the boys who did this to her been suspended?"

"I'm not at liberty to discuss consequences assigned to other students, but I can tell you there were no suspensions issued in this incident."

"I am very disturbed that none of the boys who did this were suspended," Mr. Simmons countered. "This is very serious."

"I understand your concerns," I replied. "Since I was not the one who spoke with the students I will talk further with Art Swanson, our vice-principal, and we will re-open the investigation. Perhaps there are other witnesses who have not yet been interviewed."

"Thank you, I appreciate that."

Our conversation ended politely with handshakes all around and an agreement that I would get back to him after our second investigation. The two men left the office and I sat down to process what just occurred. Thoughts kept rifling through my head. *Was this a threat or just a very concerned parent? Was I so out of touch with reality that I didn't realize the issue of lynching could be considered? What if further investigation didn't uncover that anything different happened than what we thought?* Based on what I knew, a suspension wasn't warranted. *Would Mr. Simmons and his lawyer be satisfied with that answer? If not, would they take the issue to the newspaper? Was I handling this the right way?* I needed to make sure and call the superintendent to apprise him of the conversation. I didn't sleep well that night.

~~~

As it turned out the next day Art and I conducted a far reaching investigation and an interesting discovery in our conversation with Robert.

"Robert," I asked. "When you threw that rope around Renee's neck what were you thinking? Do you know how dangerous that is?"

After much wiggling in his seat he answered. "I was teasing her and told her she was a puppy dog and I was going to walk her on a leash."

Oh my gosh I thought. "So, you *meant* to put the leash around her neck?"

"Yes."

That conversation changed our perspective on the incident and we did suspend Robert for a day. I contacted Mr. Simmons and explained the outcome of our second investigation. He thanked me for listening and although I was not at liberty to discuss the individual student consequences I did share that a day suspension was involved. He accepted the explanation and expressed that he wished the symbology of the 'lynching' to be remembered.

I don't believe there was a thought of anything nearly as serious as lynching on the part of the boys but perception is nine tenths of the law. Mr. Simmons was coming from a different historical background and we needed to respect that perspective.

NAACP Complaint!

The NAACP was ready to file a complaint against the district with the Office of Civil Rights. Nerves were running ragged at the district office. People held meetings, gathered data, and tried to figure out how to respond to the concerns. Daniel Walker, a local NAACP member wearing his exquisitely designed kufi hat, attended every school board meeting asking questions and requesting answers.

"Have you seen the NAACP's claim?" asked Mr. Walker. "That Black students in Robinson USD are overrepresented in Special Education, suspensions and expulsions?"

"They also claim that our district's Black students are underrepresented in the Gifted and Talented Education program? He continued. "This is not acceptable."

"Yes we just received the report and are very disturbed by its findings," stated Gino Lentini, a school board member.

"What do you plan to do about it?" requested Mr. Walker.

"We have formed a committee of educators from our district and we're hoping to have some NAACP members on the committee as well. This group will look into the concerns and come up with a plan of action. We've looked at our data and the claims are absolutely correct."

"May I be a member of that committee?" asked Mr. Walker

"That would be great," responded Gino. "We'd love to have you join us."

I also was excited to have the opportunity to participate on this committee by representing the elementary schools. I was looking forward to working together with the NAACP. In my three years as principal in the district I could attest to the validity of what they were stating, but I was skeptical about how this would be resolved. I hoped they really wanted answers and solutions, and were not merely looking to find fault within the district as had happened before with other groups. Robinson had received complaints in the past, some valid, and some meant to disrupt the district to further an individual or group's own cause. False concerns didn't end up with solutions.

However, I trusted the leadership of our local NAACP and wasn't surprised by their allegations. I saw evidence of it when I disaggregated data from my own site. I also experienced what, at the time, was called "soft prejudice" in the attitudes of some of the staff. Not necessarily overt or even intentional, just perhaps unaware of how they were reacting to certain students and situations.

An example of this occurred earlier in the year. Several staff members and I attended a "Beyond Diversity" training in Oakland. I was surprised at the resistance one of our teachers had to the presenter.

"I think he is just an angry young Black man. I don't have a prejudiced bone in my body and I'm offended that he challenged me when I said I don't see color when I look at my students."

I knew what she meant, but I don't think she realized what she was saying. Skin color is no different than hair color; of course you see it.

Because of comments like this and some things I observed at my site, like the large percentage of Black students that ended up in my office, I genuinely wanted to look at these concerns. It was an equity issue for these students, to be underrepresented in some areas and overrepresented in others in disproportionate numbers. I looked forward to working with the NAACP, hoping we could really make headway in solving the concerns. I wanted to know more about the school experience for our Black students. By working together, hopefully some positive changes could happen.

This all led to the beginning of conversations at our faculty meetings. We went slowly at first because it was a tender topic for many of the staff, mostly the White staff. Those teachers who attended the Beyond Diversity training shared what they had learned. Three of our teachers were Black, and we had talked before the meeting about how to engage folks in the conversation.

A big breakthrough occurred when Francie, one of the young Black teachers, stood up and stated, "I invite any of you to ask me whatever you want, anything you have wanted to know about what it's like to be Black in our society. Until we can openly talk about our differences, we won't be able to make progress in truly providing an equitable environment for our students."

Francie's comment broke the ice. Conversation sparked throughout the group. There seemed to be a fog that lifted, almost a relief that we were free to talk about this topic. Even though 35 percent of our students were Black, conversations had never really taken place about how their school experience might be different from that of White students, or students from other cultures. We decided to read some books together and discuss them as a staff. Among the books we read were *Other People's Children* by Linda Delpit and *Understanding Poverty* by Ruby Payne. Both books were excellent reads for our staff, but it was interesting how different people experienced those books. For most it was easy to discuss the circumstances of children living in poverty, and how we could support them. For many, it was more difficult when we talked about our own subconscious bias, and how we, as individuals, perceived some of our students and the culture they were raised in.

To help us deepen understanding of our Black students' experience, we decided to look more deeply into what it was like for these kids at our school. Francie, Vernice and Racquel, our three Black teachers on staff, and I met and decided that a good place to start was to organize a meeting, inviting any interested teachers and parents, to begin the conversation. We sent out a flyer advertising the event, and the positive response showed high interest in talking about this concern. Several teachers and about twenty-five parents signed up to attend the first meeting. What started as a complaint opened the door to what we hoped would be genuine conversations about race, equity and what was best for all students.

 "Change your thoughts and you change your world."
~Norman Vincent Peale

Black Student Achievement Committee

*W*e met early on a balmy Saturday morning at school. I anxiously waited in the school library with Vernice, Racquel, and Francie for the parents to arrive. They were the three teachers who had worked so hard to make this meeting happen and today was our first with the parents of the Black students at our school.

After the news came that the NAACP was threatening to file their complaint, the four of us met with several other teachers to discuss how best to plan this meeting.

"Data doesn't lie," Racquel had said. "If you look at the details it tells what's going on and everyone wants to know why. It's a complicated issue that has many layers; we need to begin to peel back this onion."

Racquel was a no-nonsense fifth-grade teacher. She had a quick wit, and a dry sense of humor, was in her forties and had raised her own son. She was very firm with her students but she deeply cared about them and they knew it. One day at the end of school I saw her chastise a student when he asked his mother to get his books from his desk.

"Those aren't your mother's books," she said. "You go get them yourself."

His mom was nodding her head as if to say, *"Thank you."*

Racquel, along with the rest of us, was looking forward to this meeting and our hope was to spark some genuine conversation. We had decided the first thing we wanted to do was talk with the parents and hear their thoughts about the report. After all, each school in our district had an Advisory Committee to create policy and support for English Learners. Perhaps Baxter would be the first school in the district to have an advisory committee to support Black Students. Who better to talk with about concerns regarding their students than the parents themselves? We sent out a letter telling the families about the contents of the report and we told them we wanted to talk with them about our concerns and work together to find solutions.

"Twenty-five parents are coming to this meeting," said Vernice excitedly. "That tells me this is an issue they want to talk about."

Vernice lived in Robinson and had taught at the school for thirty years. She had been brought up as a Southern debutante, and race was something you didn't talk about in mixed company (mixed as in Black and White) in her circles, but she felt it was time to delve into this issue, and, as a school, to support the students.

"We've had this problem for all thirty years I've been teaching at Baxter. No one has ever talked about why it's this way. The common perception has been that Black students act up more in class, get into more fights on the playground, and therefore are suspended more frequently. That may be true, but if we dig deeper we may be able to find out why and what we can do about it."

Francie spoke up, "Maybe today will open up the door for us. I'm thrilled we have so many parents coming. Several came to me personally to tell me how pleased they are about having this discussion."

Francie taught fourth grade and was in her twenties, very introspective and thoughtful. She had been teaching at Baxter for two years, was involved on many of our school improvement committees, and was thrilled to be part of this conversation.

~~~

As the parents began to arrive, I felt myself tensing up. Why? I knew most of these folks and had good relationships with them. I had sat in meetings with them about their kids, worked on committees with several of them, and just talked with others in the office. The majority of our conversations were very polite. There was the occasional misunderstanding and those could get heated, but none of those parents had signed up to come to this meeting. Why did today seem different? Was it because we were going to be talking about a subject that people could have strong feelings about? Was it because it was a subject most people felt uncomfortable being open about? Maybe it was because I was the one who had to facilitate the meeting? I had struggled with how to open and finally decided to be very straightforward in my approach. I hoped the message would be received in the way it was intended.

After welcoming everyone and doing introductions around the room, I explained why we had called the meeting and then started.

"I am a White woman in the role of principal in a school where 35 percent of our students are Black. It disturbs me to see these statistics about our students. I can't begin to say that I know what school is like for them. I haven't walked in their shoes. I need to have your help in gaining a better understanding of what it's like for them here at Baxter, what it's like for you, their parents, and how we can work together to change these statistics."

That started an enlightening discussion. We used chart paper to record comments. I facilitated, Vernice charted, and Racquel and Francie gently encouraged different parents to participate. One of the more insightful comments came from a mother whose son was one of our more academically successful fourth graders.

"In your culture," she began, "people are very decorous. One person speaks and the others listen. When that person is through talking, then another person speaks, and so on. In our culture, in our homes and in our churches, it can be more like a "shout out." Our voices weave in and out of each other's, we respond in the middle of another person's sentence, but it's not considered impolite. It's a way of affirming what the other has said. Our kids are used to this kind of interaction. When they get to school it's a different situation. They're expected to respond like you do in your culture. We teach them how to switch, but for some of them it's difficult, and some are never taught how."

As I listened, and Vernice recorded the comments, I realized I was learning the other side of the story. It caused me to reflect on how we teach our students. The majority of them are not raised in the White culture. Are we respectful of the way things are done in their cultures? Can we incorporate new teaching strategies that mirror all cultures in our school? We were starting to peel the onion.

One comment led to another. New hands went up. As we continued to talk, people were very open and honest about the issues at hand, and the vibe in the room was positive. The parents wanted to meet again and chose a name for our group, the Black Student Achievement Committee (BSAC). We decided to hold a workshop and include some middle and high school personnel. I could feel my body relax. It was encouraging to believe that once you step through a door like this, you don't go back. We were on our way to working together on an important issue at our school and in our culture.

 "Conversation is the natural way we humans think together" *~Margaret Wheatley*

Popcorn Fire Drill

*T*here's smoke in the second grade hallway!" These are words no principal ever wants to hear.

"Janet, call the fire department." My heart was racing as I hurried down the hall, past the cafeteria. What was happening?

As I turned toward the second grade classrooms, I could see smoke in the hallway. I quickly radioed back to the school office. "Tell the firemen the smoke is coming from the west end of the second grade hall, the middle hall."

Rusty, our custodian, was out of breath as he came running. "Where's that smoke coming from?"

"The second grade hall. Pull the fire alarm now. Then check what you can but be careful."

He pulled the closest fire alarm and headed toward the second grade hallway. I rushed back to the office to get the bullhorn and meet students and teachers outside the buildings.

It seemed like an eternity, but actually was less than a minute and all classrooms had been emptied and students were in single file, walking toward their evacuation spots on the yard. They were quiet and orderly, knowing how to act in a fire drill, but the teachers looked anxious. They were aware this was not a planned drill. We could hear the sirens of fire trucks as they approached our school. Thankfully they were quick responders.

Thoughts whirled in my head as I grabbed the bullhorn and made my way outside. Starting on the side of the school, I checked off each class waiting in their rows, each teacher nodding to let me know all students were accounted for. When I reached the back playground, where the last of the students were lined up, I could see two firemen already on the schoolyard.

They were talking to Rusty and two teachers, Hannah and Paula. As I approached the group I observed a demeanor that didn't fit with the immediacy of the situation. The conversation was not what I expected. Hannah was nervously laughing, her hands covering her mouth. Paula was explaining something to the firemen, gesturing in a very animated manner. "I didn't know she had put popcorn in my microwave."

Paula was telling him that she had just brought her students in from recess and settled them down to work when they noticed a smell like something was burning. As they searched the room they discovered the smell was coming from the microwave.

"I opened the door and smoke came billowing out. At first I didn't know what it was. Then I could see what I thought was a bag. It didn't look like it was on fire so I grabbed the corner and flung it into the hallway. Smoke started filling the hall and I ran back inside and called the office."

At this point two more firemen came out of the building to where we were talking.

"All is clear and safe for the students and teachers to return to their classrooms. We found a bag of burned popcorn in the middle of the hallway."

I rolled my eyes and thanked them.

After a brief conversation with the firemen about safety procedures, I turned my attention to the students and teachers waiting on the yard, using the bullhorn to thank them for the great job they'd done following our emergency procedures. I also told them that it was now safe to return to their classrooms.

I rejoined the conversation about the incident. Hannah was now wringing her hands as she talked to the firemen. "I am so sorry. How could I have been so stupid? I teach right across the hall and I use Paula's microwave all the time. I put the bag of popcorn in it at recess, and then two of my students came in upset from the yard, and I was so engrossed in helping them, I forgot about the popcorn. I can't believe I caused you to come out here for nothing."

The firemen very graciously assured Hannah that this was not the first time this kind of thing had happened, and it was much better to be safe than sorry, so they were glad we called them. They suggested that perhaps next time she put popcorn in the microwave she set a timer or do something to remind herself, so this wouldn't happen again.

We all felt relieved and decided to wait until lunchtime to officially let the rest of the staff know the whole story of the unexpected fire drill. For now, Hannah had provided an opportunity to check off that box showing a completed fire drill for the month of May.

THE SEVENTH INNING

DIFFICULT DECISIONS ARE MADE DAILY!

Report to CPS!

*A*s I entered the office that morning, I saw her. She looked to be in her late twenties. She had a slight build with curly, long brown hair. She wore jeans, a puffy maroon jacket and high brown boots. Her eyes were red and swollen and looked as if she had been crying for quite some time. I turned to her.

"You look upset. Is there something I can help you with?"

"Yes, I am upset." She choked up as she started to speak.

I escorted her into my office. She sat down in one of the chairs at the round table and I sat next to her. By this time she was almost sobbing. I put my hand on her arm to try to calm her so she could talk.

She took a deep breath and began to speak. "Yesterday, when I picked my son up from the after school program, he let me know that he had told his teacher I hit him on his legs. He said she kept asking questions about whether it left a mark, and did he have a mark on him right now. She was forcing him to answer these questions and she made him show her his legs. I know that teachers have to report these conversations with students, so I know that she had to call Child Protective Services (CPS). I am so worried that the police are going to come and take my son away. I'm in a program at the local college to become a peace officer, and this could cost me all that I have worked for. I'm a good mother. I don't want his teacher to think I beat my child, because I don't. I did hit him on the leg one time. I have neuropathy in my legs and I was sitting on the couch. He was on the floor having a temper tantrum. He kept kicking his legs out and his legs kept hitting mine so I hit him on the leg and yelled at him to stop because he was hurting me. But I don't beat him. He has those bruises on his legs because he is a normal seven year old boy and runs and falls down a lot."

She was talking so fast I put my hand on her arm again, just to slow her down. "First of all, don't worry about someone taking your son away. For one thing the police aren't going to come and take Jacob away because of one phone call. There has to be a long history of abuse before that would happen, and that's not true in your case."

Actually I knew very little about this family. Jacob was new to our school this year, so I didn't know if there was a history of abuse or not. But I wanted to calm her down.

"As for the teacher, she knows you, you have been volunteering in her classroom every week all year, she sees how you act with your son, and she knows you're a good mother. Please don't worry about her thinking badly of you."

A small smile began to appear on her face.

I continued. "As far as a report to CPS, yes, if a student tells a teacher that someone hit him that teacher is obligated, as a mandated reporter, to make a report."

Her eyes widened again as she looked at me.

"What will most likely happen is that you will receive a phone call from CPS and if you do, just tell them what you told me. They will understand. They are concerned about abusive situations, not about what you just described to me."

Her shoulders began to relax; she breathed a sigh of relief and then explained. "My son is very worried about coming to school today. You see, I was so upset with him last night for saying that to his teacher that I told him the police could come and take him away from us."

Oh my god! I thought. I looked at my watch. It was 8:05 a.m.

"Where's your son right now?"

"He's at home with his father, because my husband brings him to school."

"I'd like you to go home right now and talk to your son before he comes here. Please reassure him that the police are not going to come and take him away from you and your husband. Also, please let him know that he did the right thing telling a safe adult about what happened. We have been holding child safety programs here at school and the students have been told that if someone is doing something that doesn't feel right to them, they should let a safe adult know about it. I understand how you feel, but in theory, he was exercising the power he was taught about in the program."

She agreed to go talk with her son and we went out of the office together. As she walked toward her car, I headed to Jacob's classroom to find his teacher. She was a young, new substitute at the school; she had never taught before and had been very nervous about making this CPS report. She was grading papers in the classroom when I found her.

"Hi Stacey, I want to fill you in on the CPS report and my conversation with Jacob's mother."

"Thanks for coming by, I was so nervous about making that report. I wasn't sure if it was the right thing to do. They didn't talk about that in my credential program at college."

"I know, none of us like to make that phone call but you absolutely did the right thing. We don't have any way of knowing if other reports have been made. Sometimes when CPS follows up they find that it was a false accusation or a one time minor circumstance and they talk to the parent(s) and that's the end of it. But other times there is a long string of complaints and they have to take action. We don't know that history so our job is to notify CPS."

This is one of the painful decisions faced by a mandated reporter. You would never choose to separate a child from their parent, but sometimes you need to do what you think is best to keep a child safe.

In this case it ended well. There was no CPS file history, and life settled down for Jacob and his mother.

Read Across America

_T_he box arrived from the Oriental Trading Company with seventy-five hats in it. They were stovepipe hats, just like the ones worn in the book, _Cat in The Hat_. There was every color combination imaginable: orange and white striped, red and black-striped, and green and yellow striped hats.

"I'll take that one," announced Barry. "Red and black are Mickey Mouse colors."

Barry was wearing a Mickey Mouse t-shirt and loose baggy pants with an elastic waist. His pants had small Mickey Mouses all over them. They looked like pajama bottoms.

That was fitting, for today was _Read Across America Day_. All adults on campus got to pick a stovepipe hat to wear that day. They could dress as casually as they wished. I had known this day was coming, so while on vacation in Disneyland I had bought a huge red and white striped hat. It looked just like the one in _The Cat in the Hat_ except it had big Mickey Mouse ears on it. I was thrilled to wear it for the first time; I think I was more excited about this day than the students!

"Here's what I love about _Read Across America Day_," Barry enthused, "We have nothing but reading going on all day."

"Yep, what could be better for our students?"

He stuffed a bunch of paper inside his red and black striped hat to make it stand up straight on his head and then he penguin-marched his way back to his classroom, looking back at me laughing.

Teacher's had reading activities planned all day for their students, and we had invited a Mystery Reader for each classroom. I was anxious to be part of the activities.

"Janet, I'll be back later. I'm going to visit classrooms and see how our Mystery Readers are doing." I donned my red and white striped hat. "Call my cell if you need me."

My first stop was the kindergarten room. What a treat! In the front of the class was Assistant Superintendent of Human Resources, Wayne Russell, sitting in a kindergarten-sized chair, wearing one of our purple and yellow striped hats. What made me smile was that he hadn't stuffed the hat with any paper so, as it sat on his head, half of it drooped over on one side. He wore a white shirt and loosened tie, his shirtsleeves were rolled up, and his glasses were perched on the tip of his nose. He was reading the book, *"Hand, Hand, Fingers, Thumb."* Twenty kids, aged five and six, were all wearing red and white striped paper stove-pipe hats they had made, and were sitting on the rug, their eyes glued to him as he read *"Hands, hands, fingers thumb, dum ditty, dum ditty, dum dum dum."* Pretty soon, all the kids were repeating this stanza every time Wayne came to it in the book. Wayne's voice became more animated each time he read it. The kids were eating it up and developing pre-reading skills at the same time. I loved it! I think he did too!

I left kindergarten and made my way down the hall to Barry's third-grade classroom. Here was another treat! The students were all wearing pajamas and had brought their sleeping bags and stuffed animals. They had pushed all the desks and chairs out of the way to the sides of the room and spread out their bags on the floor. It looked like a gigantic slumber party.

One of our bus drivers, Leonore Jolley, was reading *Go, Dog, Go!* Leonore was a large woman with an infectious smile. Her body spilled over onto the sides of the small chair she was sitting on, but that didn't make any difference. She was the type of person who had a way of making each kid feel special even as she disciplined them on the bus to and from school. The students were all sitting or lying down on their sleeping bags, clutching those favorite stuffed animals, eyes fixated on Leonore as she read. *"Stop, dogs, stop, the light is red. Go, dogs, go, it's green ahead."* Several students had the same book in front of them and were reading along with Leonore. I had goose bumps on my arms watching the students enjoying reading this way.

I visited several more rooms. We had district dignitaries, parents, and community members all serving as Mystery Readers. Even my college aged daughter and two of her friends were reading in classrooms. It was rewarding to see such a collaboration of adults from many walks of life volunteering to come in and read with students.

The last event of the day was held in the Multi-Use Room. The cafeteria tables were stretched out from the side walls and as students entered they filled in both sides. We managed to stuff almost 600 students into that room.

Our last Mystery Guest of the day was about to take the floor. I took the microphone on stage to introduce him.

"Boys and girls, let's give a big round of applause for Rusty Franklin, who will read *"Green Eggs and Ham."* The auditorium broke out in wild applause. Cheering could be heard from all corners of the room. The students were ecstatic. Pretty soon you could hear, "Rus-tee, Rus-tee, Rus-tee!" as they chanted for him to come out.

The kids knew and loved Rusty, our head custodian. He appeared wearing a red and white striped stovepipe hat stuffed with paper so it stood very tall. His grey sweats, big red bow tied around his neck, and grey tail pinned to the back of his sweats made him look just like the *Cat in the Hat.* He walked among the tables with the book in his hands, reading with the ease of an experienced storyteller. *"Do you like green eggs and ham? I do not like them Sam I am. I do not like green eggs and ham."* The kids loved it!

~~~

Read Across America Day was a huge success. The Mystery Readers shared their pleasure and appreciation about being asked to come to read stories and requested to be asked back next year. The students were abuzz on the playground, at recess and lunch, sharing stories of what happened in their classrooms. We all had a fabulous day. What a wonderful way to get kids excited about reading!

 "Celebrate what you want to see more of." *~Tom Peters*

Was it Really a Knife?

$\mathcal{I}$t was the end of the day, and after the previous afternoon's encounter with Mr. Clark, the vice-principal and I watched Orlando carefully as he left the building. He was chatting and laughing with other students as they walked towards the street. Orlando Clark was a fourth grader with curly brown hair, big brown eyes and an engaging smile. He was smaller and younger than most boys in his class. He sat on the dangerous edge of being the class clown, mostly because he seemed to crave the attention his behavior generated from his classmates.

Orlando always walked home from school, so he waved goodbye to his buddies as they veered off toward the waiting school buses. Orlando turned in the opposite direction and walked to the corner. He waited for the green light. This was the way he always walked home. He crossed at the signal, walked past the park, and continued towards Hanford Street, where he stopped at the ice cream truck parked at the curb. Many of the kids from our school, as well as the middle school, liked to stop to buy ice cream and candy on their way home.

We stood there anticipating what we might see. As expected, there was Orlando's father. He was across the street waiting for his son. We were hoping he might have come just to give Orlando a ride home but, as we suspected, that didn't seem to be the case. He was outside his car when he greeted the boy. They talked for a bit and then Mr. Clark turned around and looked at the school. He reached into his pocket, then turned back around with his back again to the school, he handed something to Orlando, got into his car and drove away. Orlando put his hand in his pocket, looked around for a moment and then continued walking down the street.

Mr. Clark was a concerned father but he had a very short fuse, which made him quick to jump to conclusions and frequently make unwarranted accusations. A few days ago he had shared with us that some kids were bullying Orlando. Since then we had been working together to try to resolve the problem, but the process was not moving fast enough for Mr. Clark. He had made that obvious in yesterday's meeting.

I had been in my office when he stormed past the Office Manager and in to see me. There was a man with him I recognized as Orlando's uncle. Alarmed at the intensity with which he spoke, and very uncomfortable about being inside the office with him, I quickly got up and walked towards the doorway to greet him.

"Why haven't you done anything to stop Orlando from being bullied?" he demanded in a combative voice. "Now it's happening after school too, and I'm sick and tired of it."

"Actually," I responded, "when we talked with Orlando he was reluctant to tell us who had been bothering him so we have been interviewing his friends, hoping they might provide information for us."

Dad took a few steps forward and glared down at me. He was now about twelve inches from my face. I could feel my heart starting to beat faster as he raised his voice even more. I took a step to the side and further away from him.

"Well that's not fast enough for me. I'm gonna arm my son with a knife and send him to school with it tomorrow. Then he can take care of whoever it is once and for all."

I looked at him alarmed. He was intense and frightening. My mind was racing as fast as my heart. I was thinking about my personal safety as I slipped past him and pretended to reach for something outside my office door and in clearer view of others.

"Mr. Clark. You know you can't do that. You know if that happened, it could cause Orlando to be expelled from school, and that wouldn't be fair to him."

"I don't care! I don't want him at this school any more anyway. We're gonna take care of this ourselves." Then he turned around and thundered away from the office.

Orlando's uncle stopped for a moment. "I'm so sorry this happened. I tried to talk sense into him. I hope he doesn't do it, but I don't know if I can stop him."

After they left I slumped down in my chair and let out a huge sigh. Our office manager, Janet, came in and brought me a cup of tea.

"Thanks Janet, I needed that."

"That scared the heck out of me," she said. "He's always been a big bully but I've never seen him that bad."

After I calmed down I contacted the superintendent to alert him about the situation. I told him how upset Orlando's father was and how he had acted with me.

"Do you want someone from the district to be at your school in the morning tomorrow?" Don asked."

"No, I think we're okay, my VP will be there and we have enough other staff to support us if his father does anything bizarre."

"Well, make sure to have someone look inside Orlando's backpack before he goes to class to make sure there is no weapon in there, and be sure to call us if anything happens and you need extra support."

That conversation with Don made me feel a little better.

~~~

The next morning when Orlando arrived at school, I met him outside and asked him to come into my office for a minute.

"You can leave your backpack in the front while we talk," I said. I had previously asked Janet to check it thoroughly to make sure there were no weapons inside.

We talked again about what was happening.

"I spoke with your father yesterday, he's very concerned about you feeling safe at school."

"I wish he would just let me take care of this myself. I don't have any problems at school, it's after school on the way home."

"Is the problem with a student here at Baxter?"

"I don't want to say who it is but I'm ignoring them and it is getting better."

"Have you explained this to your father?"

"I don't like to talk to him about it because he gets so mad and it embarrasses me when he comes down to school like that."

I prodded again but he didn't want to tell me who it was that was bothering him. I wasn't sure I believed him when he said it was getting better. He wouldn't look at me when he was talking; he just looked down at the floor. I assured him that we wanted to make sure he was safe and to please be sure to tell his teacher or me if anyone bothered him at school. He said he would.

After our chat, I sent Orlando back to his classroom and the rest of the day went smoothly. No incidents occurred until the moment after school when we saw his father across the street. We assumed, after his threats, that it may have been a knife or some kind of weapon that he handed to his son. This had now become a much bigger situation than we wanted to handle by ourselves so we contacted the police. We provided a description of Orlando and explained the situation. They said they would check it out.

A couple of hours later the police followed up with us. They had located Orlando on his way home and shadowed him to a local convenience store where he joined up with some other kids. The kids all seemed to know each other and there didn't appear to be any problems, so the police left and went to Orlando's home to talk with his father. Sure enough Dad admitted he had handed his son a knife for protection. The police assured us they had talked with Mr. Clark about the dangers of arming his son with a weapon and let us know they would keep an eye on the situation.

That didn't become necessary because Orlando never returned to school. We discovered he and his father had left the neighborhood where they had been living with relatives. I felt sad that we didn't get to say goodbye to Orlando and he didn't have an opportunity for closure with his teacher and classmates. I think with some time we would have been able to help Orlando deal with his tormenters. It was disappointing to think that our probing had driven Mr. Clark to take his son away. Our goal had not been to judge but to try to keep his son safe.

 "Education is the most powerful weapon which you can use to change the world." *~Nelson Mandela*

Homeless in Fifth Grade

*W*hile I was attending a school district meeting with Don, our superintendent, my office secretary called. She said Gabriela Roberts was waiting in the school office.

"Oh my god, I can't believe it! Please tell her to wait, I'll be there in 5 minutes."

I stopped what I was doing and apologized to Don. I had been waiting for this mother to show up for weeks, so I quickly headed back to school. I knew he would understand.

She was sitting in the office when I arrived. The youngish woman appeared very different from what I expected of a homeless mother. She was nicely dressed, with dark leather boots, a hip looking sweater and stylish shoulder-length, wavy brown hair. She carried a new black Gucci handbag and an iPhone and she greeted me with a smile.

~~~

We'd been trying for several weeks to arrange this meeting. Ms. Roberts had evaded us for a long time. In the 87 days since school started Caroline, her fifth grade daughter, had been absent 20 days and tardy another 21 days. She had missed 25 percent of school. We had sent two letters stating our concerns and never heard back from anyone. I had reviewed her attendance record and could see this had been a pattern ever since kindergarten. Caroline had attended 7 different schools, and her record of absences and tardies in the past looked similar to this year.

Mom had agreed to meet this afternoon but had not committed to a time. I had been afraid she wouldn't show up but here she was and I wasn't going to miss meeting with her.

"Welcome, Gabriela. I'm Jane Blomstrand, principal, I'm so happy you could come in to meet me today. Let's go down to my office."

Gabriela followed me and we sat down at the round conference table. I had Caroline's file in front of me. She smiled and set her Gucci bag down on the floor.

"I wanted to talk with you about Caroline's attendance record."

"I know, she's had a lot of absences. I can explain that. Caroline and I both have been sick a lot this year. She had a bad case of the flu in November and for several days she was in bed."

"But she's also been tardy 19 times."

"Well, when she started to get better, I let her sleep in in the morning, and when she woke up then I would bring her to school. I figured it was better for her to be at school for at least half the day than not at all. That way the school would still get their money and she wouldn't miss all day."

"But, this has been a pattern ever since she was in kindergarten." I showed her our spreadsheet revealing Caroline's attendance record since kindergarten.

She looked at the spreadsheet for a while. "Oh, I didn't realize she'd been in that many schools."

"I also wanted to check on your current address. When we mailed her test scores to you, the envelope came back to us marked, 'not at this address.'"

"Oh yes, well there was a mold problem in that house, and we had to move out last August so they could fix it, and then when it was repaired the owner said she wasn't going to rent to us anymore. We're staying in the room of a friend's house now but he told us we have to find another place to live, and I can't use his address because he doesn't want to be responsible for our mail, so we had to get a P.O. Box."

Listening to this I sighed internally. "Can you provide me with the address of where you're staying now, and your P.O. Box? That way when we need to send you materials regarding Caroline you'll receive them?"

"Sure, but I'm trying to find another place on Craigslist in between jobs"

"Where do you work?"

"Anywhere I can find it. I'm a nanny, I cook and clean, and sometimes I paint houses. I do a lot of things depending on what the job is."

"How do you find your work?"

"On Craigslist. Most of my jobs are down in the wealthier area of the county. They pay very well down there you know. That's why Caroline is tardy so much. If I have a nanny job there I need to get those kids to school first, so I can't take Caroline until after I drop the other kids off. Some of my other jobs start at 6:00 in the morning, so I either have to take Caroline with me, or drop her off at Starbucks. She has a card so she can get something to eat and drink, and wait there until school is ready to start, and then she walks to school from the coffee shop."

I sighed. I was thinking of this little girl sitting by herself in a coffee shop, for two hours in the morning, waiting for school to start. How lonely that must feel.

"What about after school? On the days when you are working late, what does Caroline do?"

"She has her card to Starbucks and another one at McDonalds. She walks to either place to get something to eat. Then she usually goes to the library and stays there until I pick her up."

Oh my, I thought, this woman was using the downtown area as her babysitter before and after school. As appalling as I thought that situation was, I had to appreciate her ingenuity. She knew it was a relatively safe community, which is why she tried her best to keep her daughter in school here. She arranged for food cards and safe places for Caroline to stay. I thought of my own daughter and how that situation would be for her.

"Do you know we have a private, after school day care right here at school? If you'd like I can check with the director to see if they provide scholarships."

"Oh I had no idea. That would be wonderful. Thank you so much."

We talked some more about the importance of Caroline being at school and what else we could offer in support.

"I also have the name of an advocate at our county office of education. She helps people who are temporarily out of a home and can provide you with many services."

"Oh thank you, that would be very helpful," responded Mrs. Roberts.

"I would also like to set up a Student Support Team meeting here at school, we call it an SST. A group of us; her teacher, the school counselor, and you and I would get together to collaborate on how to best support Caroline, are you okay with that?"

Mom agreed and luckily, we were able to arrange to meet the next day. Mom thanked me profusely for understanding her situation and listening to her. Then she picked up her iPhone and Gucci bag and left.

I was conflicted about this situation. Could we believe Mom's stories? We were told she had a history of being untruthful to other school officials. I could see from her record this was not a new situation. Other schools had tried to help.

I tried to focus on what was best for Caroline. But what was best for Caroline? If we got the police and Child Protective Services involved would we risk her being taken away from her mother? What exactly would be in her best interests?

Caroline's attendance did improve for the remainder of the year. She completed fifth grade and graduated to middle school.

Every once in a while in the next couple of years when I was in the coffee shop late in the afternoon I would still see Caroline and know she was waiting to be picked up by her mother.

---

66 **"I'm a very strong believer in listening and learning from others." ~Ruth Bader Ginsberg**

Reading Recovery

*G*ina was the last of six kindergarten teachers to give me her answer, and it was "yes!" Excellent news! I gave her a big hug. Now all six kindergarten teachers were on board to be part of our new program. We were training them in an intense reading intervention program called Reading Recovery. Once trained, each would partner with a first grade class, providing one-on-one support to our most struggling readers. It had taken a chunk of our school intervention money and a lot of maneuvering with the district office to get approval to implement this program.

"Oh Gina, I'm so excited. I know you had to put a lot of thought into this decision. It's not easy to volunteer your time one day a week after school when you have a family to care for."

"No, it's not, but Joe and I thought a lot about it and we were able to work out child care. I think this program could make a big difference for our first graders, and I really want to be part of it."

Inside I was jumping for joy. There were so many parts to making this program work. Each of our kindergarten teachers would be getting specific training at a local university in teaching reading. This could help make them more effective teachers, not only with the first graders, but also with their own kindergarten students.

"Now our next step is to decide which first graders we're going to ask to participate in the six week demonstration part of the class."

Gina and I talked for a bit. This would be tricky. The program required a semester long training. Each teacher would drive a student to class one time for a demonstration lesson after which the instructor required the teacher only, to stay for the remainder of the class. The university was 45 minutes away.

"We'll have to consider all the logistics involved in the demonstration lessons," I mentioned. "And find six parents who will agree to have their child participate."

"I talked to Maria's dad just to see what his reaction would be," responded Gina. "He said for sure he'd like to have Maria participate and had no problem with us driving her to and from the university on her day. I think as a school board member he is excited that we are implementing this program."

"That's great. If each of you can select one student from your class for your demo lesson we'll be all set. Those six parents will need to fill out field trip permission forms."

"Perfect, that makes sense. So, I know we have to stay for the rest of the class after the demo lesson, what will the students do during that time?" asked Gina.

"Well, what if I picked up each student after their demo lesson and drove them home? That would be six different Mondays, I could do that."

We presented this idea to the other teachers and they all agreed.

For me, it was a bonus. Every Monday when I picked up a student, we would take a short campus tour and visit the bookstore where we would buy a small souvenir of their "college visit." I was looking forward to that one-on-one time with each student. I could talk to them about their ideas for the future and where they would like to go to college.

In the meantime there were many questions to be answered. Would we have trouble convincing parents of the value in letting their kids be part of this program? How would we collect long-term data on the participating students and their future reading success? What about the teacher's union contract? Could we pay the teachers for the extra 4 hours of class every Monday evening for five months plus mileage? There were lots of things to think about. Now that the plan was becoming a reality my head was swimming with ideas. I needed to meet with Anna.

Anna was head of curriculum at our district office. She and I had already talked about Reading Recovery as a possibility and brainstormed together before I approached the teachers. I called to tell her all the teachers had agreed to participate and we set up a meeting for the next morning.

I arrived early. "Anna, I'm so excited! I can't believe all of the six kinder teachers are able to be part of the program. Can you and I just talk through this to make sure I'm not forgetting any important details?"

"That's great news! Why don't you run your ideas by me, ask me questions, then we'll go from there."

Anna and I spent the next three hours talking about how this was going to work. What had started out as an idea a year before was now about to be implemented. Our school would have six kindergarten teachers instruct their usual a.m or p.m. class, then provide targeted reading instruction for struggling first-graders the other half of their day. With six first grade classes, thirty more kids each year would have a better head start at achieving academic success.

~~~

As I think about it now, getting all six kindergarten teachers to commit to that training was absolutely critical. If even one of them had been unable to participate in the program as we designed it, it wouldn't have happened. At the time I was a new, naïve principal who came up with an idea to support struggling readers and figured everyone else would be just as excited about implementing it as I was.

And the incredible part was these remarkable, dedicated teachers actually made it happen!

 "There are those who look at things the way they are and ask why. I dream of things that never were, and ask why not?" *~John Fitzgerald Kennedy*

Preparing for Outdoor Ed Camp

She was a friendly little 11-year-old with almond shaped eyes; light brown hair that fell in wispy curls around her face, a small flat nose, and unusually small ears. Ruby was adorable. She loved being in school, maybe not always following the rules, and maybe a little too impulsive, but being around her peers was the highlight of Ruby's day. She loved reading books with her teacher and playing tetherball on the playground.

Today Ruby had trouble paying attention to Julie Carson, her teacher.

"Ruby, you need to go back to your seat to finish your math paper before we go into the other classrooms."

"I'm finished."

"Ruby, come over here, I don't see your answer to number 2 and number 4. Come on back and we'll finish it together."

Ruby returned to her seat and she and Julie finished the paper together.

"I'm nervous to go into classrooms today," Ruby said as she quietly reached over and squeezed Julie's hand.

"I know, Ruby, but you'll do very well. They'll be so excited to hear what you and I have to tell them. Just think about what we've practiced together. You'll be wonderful."

Ruby and her teacher were going to visit all the fifth grade classrooms today, in preparation for Outdoor Education camp. In fifth grade all the kids had the opportunity to attend this 5-day overnight camp and Ruby would be attending with the other students for one of the nights, maybe all four depending on the success of the first one. Ruby has Down Syndrome and she and Mrs. Carson were going to talk to the other students about what Down Syndrome is, what causes it, and how a person who has Down Syndrome may do some things differently.

I had attended one of Ruby's presentations as she and Julie shared their knowledge of her disability, and goosebumps covered my arms throughout. I was amazed to watch this little girl talk in front of her peers about something that was different about herself. Together they had researched Down Syndrome and prepared a summary of talking points and a demonstration of the skills she wanted to share with her classmates.

I was looking forward to attending this one and, when I walked into the fifth grade classroom, Ruby was already seated on a bar stool in front of the students, her teacher standing next to her. Julie would ask a question, prompting Ruby to respond with information they had prepared. Her sentences were short and Julie would fill in the needed information.

"Ruby," asked Julie, "can you tell the class what Down Syndrome is?"

"I have another chromosome," answered Ruby. She lowered her head laughing as she responded to the question.

"Yes, that's right," continued Julie. "You have a different mix of chromosomes than most people and that's why some may think you look a little different than many other kids. Can you tell the class what you like to do on the playground like everyone else?"

"I like to play tetherball," Ruby answered excitedly as she swung her arm out as if hitting a ball.

They talked more about all the things she could do like everyone else, and some of the things that were harder for her. After the presentation Ruby and Julie invited students in the class to ask questions. As most of them had been in school with Ruby since kindergarten they knew her, but many hadn't been in class with her for several years so they had lots of questions.

"I remember when we were in first grade together and you wouldn't talk to the other kids. You did a great job today," said Peter.

"What is your favorite book to read?" asked Sophie.

"Does it feel different having another chromosome?" asked Olivia.

They were all interested, amazed, and impressed by the newly recognized abilities she possessed.

I walked away from the presentation believing Ruby would have an incredible time at fifth grade camp, and every student's experience at camp would be enriched from having shared Outdoor Education with Ruby.

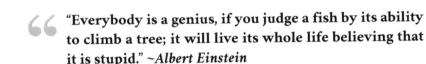

"Everybody is a genius, if you judge a fish by its ability to climb a tree; it will live its whole life believing that it is stupid." ~*Albert Einstein*

The Parking Lot Fight

*S*arah Thomas arrived at Back to School Night late. She was unable to find a place to park in the school parking lot. Not wanting to park down the street, making her even later to the classroom, she looked around and saw a small Honda Civic. The owner of that car was probably also in a classroom and would be coming out at the same time. She could hurry out and be gone by the time they wanted to leave. Figuring it would be okay to double-park; she pulled her car up behind the blue Honda and hustled off to her son's classroom.

~~~

After Back to School Night ended and Sarah was leaving, she saw her friend, Adrienne.

"Hey Adrienne, I haven't seen you in ages, how are you? How are Billy and Markie doing? Who are their teachers this year?

Sarah continued her conversation, catching up on the latest with Adrienne and her family. After about 20 minutes she remembered she had double-parked.

"Oh my god, I'm so sorry, Adrienne. I forgot I double-parked. I've got to get out to the parking lot."

As she approached her car she saw a woman peering into the window.

"Why are you looking inside my car?"

The other woman's response was very heated. "This is your car? Why in the hell did you double park behind me? And you're not even out here when Back to School Night is over. I have to get home to a babysitter and I've been waiting for half an hour. Now you come strolling out here as if nothing's happened. Don't you have any consideration for anyone else? "

That response raised Sarah's hackles, and she started yelling at the woman. Realizing she was in the wrong, had she just apologized, gotten into her car and driven off, it probably would have ended the situation. But now the two women were screaming at each other in the school parking lot in full view of other parents and children.

"Don't you yell at me like that."

"Well get your car out of my way, you inconsiderate b----." The other woman continued yelling at Sarah as she stormed over to the trunk of her car.

Sarah, who had a vivid imagination and watched too many police shows on television, feared the woman might become violent and yelled to others around her, "Watch out, this woman might have a gun!"

The other woman whipped around. "What is the matter with you? I'm getting my jacket out of my trunk because I'm cold. Are you insane? Get your car out of my way."

Hearing the fighting and worried that something terrible might erupt, another parent had quietly called the police on her cell phone and rushed into the office to alert me that there was a fight in the parking lot. The vice-principal and I both hustled out to where we saw a cluster of parents. As we arrived on the scene, a police car pulled up and two officers hopped out.

What we saw were two women screaming at each other with a group of parents and students standing by watching. One father was doing his best to calm them down.

When they saw the police both women started talking as loud and fast as they could, each telling their side of the story.

"Whoa, whoa, whoa, calm down a minute. Whose car is this?" the policeman asked, pointing to Sarah's car.

"That's my car."

"Well Ma'am, please move it over there," pointing to an empty parking spot, "and go wait for us in the school office."

"But officer, she was screaming at me, and threatening and yelling obscenities at me. I want her arrested."

"Ma'am, we will have a chance to hear your side of this story, but first please move your car out of this woman's way."

Begrudgingly, Sarah obliged and the policeman asked if the vice-principal or I would accompany her to the school office. "Would you please keep her occupied until we finish our interview here? Then we'll come into the office and meet with her? We just want them separated right now."

Gaspar Renati, our vice-principal, escorted Sarah into the office, and I stayed behind as the police interviewed the other woman. After the police concluded their questions and calmed the women down they both declined to press charges. Sarah apologized and agreed that she should not have double-parked in the first place. What should have been a civil resolution to the problem ended up extending Back to School night almost an hour for many of us.

~~~

If all us educators had to be concerned about were students and their education, our job would be relatively stress-free. Back to School Night may not have ended as we anticipated; but luckily most who attended had no idea of the drama that surfaced in the school parking lot after they left.

"Children have never been very good at listening to their elders, but they have never failed to imitate them" ~*James Baldwin*

Sexual Harassment

*I*t all began as innocent flirtation, at least that's what Robin thought. Robin was a young, attractive, first year kindergarten teacher at Baxter, and she wanted to be on the good side of Rusty, our custodian. Rusty had been at the school for many years and knew where everything was stashed. He had the power to provide her with "extras" if she needed them for her classroom. From time to time she would bring in gift certificates to Burger King for Rusty to thank him for helping her. They hit it off very well.

Rusty liked to find excuses to hang out near Robin's room. She was bubbly, friendly and fun to be with. She always joked around with him, and those minor flirtations fed his ego. Rusty was a body builder, a good-looking guy with a twinkle in his eye and an engaging smile. He was married and had two children at Baxter, but he certainly appreciated the attention when female teachers joked around with him.

While he loved being the center of attention and had great relationships with students, he was inconsistent when caring for the school. The maintenance guys in the district knew Rusty as the custodian who had carved out a little niche in the back storeroom of the cafeteria. He had confiscated an old Barcalounger from the dump, and an old TV set from his house, and squeezed them into this storeroom. In the past, whenever Rusty wasn't visible in classrooms or cleaning the cafeteria, they knew where to look for him. He had grumbled a lot when we found another use for that storeroom.

One day the flirtations took a turn. The school day was over and Robin walked her kindergartners out to the front of the school. Most of them boarded the big yellow bus; a few met family members who drove up and waited by the curb behind the bus. Robin always kept the non-bus students by her side so she could walk them to meet whoever was picking them up. It was important to make sure she knew whom they were getting into the car with before she let them out of her care.

On this afternoon she waved goodbye to the last student and walked back into her classroom. There was always work to be done after the students left for the day; materials needed to be prepared for the snowman they'd be making tomorrow.

She was in the back storeroom of her classroom looking for the paper she needed so didn't hear the storeroom door click shut. As she was reaching up to the highest shelf she felt something behind her. She turned around to come face to face with Rusty. He reached an arm around her waist and tried to pull her closer to him. She pushed him away.

"What the hell are you doing? Get out of here."

"Okay. Okay, I thought we were on the same page, I guess not."

Rusty left the room and Robin sat down on a stool. Tears rolled down her cheeks. Her shoulders started shaking. She stayed there for about 15 minutes, wanting to make sure he was far away. What had just happened? They were both married. He had kids at the school. She thought they had a great, friendly relationship. They joked around together but she certainly didn't give him any other messages. What made him think that behavior was okay?

The next day, Robin came to me with this story. Her lips were quivering as she related the details.

"It was awful. I don't know what he thought?" she said as tears rolled down her cheeks. "He and I always joked around with each other, but so did lots of other people on our staff."

I put my hand on her arm and handed her a tissue. "I understand," I said. "That must have been very upsetting. It's absolutely not okay. When you go home tonight I need you to write up a narrative of exactly what happened including what he said. I will need to talk with Cathy Grandlin, our new Superintendent of Human Resources and then with Rusty.

In my conversation with Cathy, she advised me to make an official report and walked me through the process. She also wanted me to investigate Rusty's relationship with other females on campus.

~~~

This was just the beginning of what turned out to be a lengthy investigation and a sexual harassment case involving six female staff members. I was distressed that, as closely as I worked together with the staff, I was unaware so many female staff members had been subjected to Rusty's unwanted advances. They each had dealt with it in their own private way.

At the end of our investigation we were ready to provide details of the case to the school board. We prepared a thorough presentation and all the women were prepared to speak at a board meeting and share their stories.

The night of the meeting arrived. We assembled in the HR office with the director for moral support, and to make sure final preparations were in place.

"Are you ladies all ready for your testimonies?" asked Cathy.

"Yep, we can present a case that will for sure make the district dismisses him," stated Robin.

Everyone was confident the results of tonight would end Rusty's work in the district. A sexual harasser had no place working in a school. The female teachers would not have to face him anymore. Nervous chatter filled the room.

Testimony was given; school board members listened and asked questions. After a couple of hours they ended the hearing and went behind closed doors to deliberate. We retreated to the HR office and waited in anticipation. There was lots of nervous chatter.

"Robin, you did a good job."

"Diane, did you see the disgusted look on that female school board member's face when you told them how he put his hand down the back of your pants? I think she was appalled as she should have been."

"I didn't like what our cafeteria worker, Rita said about our staff being friendly and always joking around with each other. It made it sound like this was no big deal."

After what seemed like ages, but was actually no more than an hour, the board members returned to present their findings and the consequences for Rusty.

The results were a slap in the face for these six women. He was given two weeks off work with no pay and reassigned to work at the high school. We were all aghast.

"You've got to be kidding," exclaimed Janet. "That's it? He's allowed to come back to work, and at the high school where there is a campus full of young females!"

"That's disgusting, that's like a reward for him."

Most of us were speechless. We all left in disbelief. I was worried about Robin arriving home safely after seeing her speed off in her truck.

The end result was that the women ended up filing a suit against the district, which resulted in the payout of a substantial amount of money. Since Rusty had been reassigned to the high school they would not have to see him any more and we ended up with a substitute custodian for the last few months of the school year. If this had happened in today's climate of the "Me Too" movement I believe the right decision would have been made. Rusty would have been fired and that money would have been used for instruction.

The Boo Boo Kit

Tiffany Allen and her friends liked to play in the kindergarten yard at recess. In their favorite game they were "Kittens" and every day they selected a different name for themselves. Today, Tiffany was "Mittens," a black kitten with white paws. As they were running and chasing each other, Samantha reached out to grab Tiffany and accidentally scratched her neck. It was a simple scratch that broke the skin but did not bleed, and Tiffany ran crying to her teacher, Gina Winter.

Gina followed typical accident procedure and sent Tiffany to the office to get a Band-Aid. Janet, our office manager, put the Band-Aid on her scratch and called home to let the parents know what had happened. Tiffany's mother wanted to know if the wound was cleaned or if any antiseptic was used. Janet advised her that district policy prohibited schools from dispensing medications or using treatments other than ice and Band-Aids without parental permission. She assured Mrs. Allen the Band-Aid seemed to take care of her daughter's needs, and Tiffany was happily back in her classroom.

Within an hour Tiffany's father called. He was upset and wanted to talk with the principal.

"My daughter was badly scratched today on the playground and I want to know why no one cleaned her wound and put something like Neosporin on it."

"Sir, we're not allowed to clean wounds or put antiseptic on them without parental permission. We're not always aware what children are allergic to and don't want to take any chances of aggravating an allergy. In this case, there was no blood to wipe off, and ice didn't seem necessary, so our office decided the best first aid was to cover the wound with a Band-Aid."

"Well, I'm not happy with that kind of treatment. It should have been cleaned off and antiseptic put on. What do I have to do to make sure this doesn't happen again?"

"We would need to have written permission from you and her mother stating the kind of treatment you want Tiffany to receive."

"I'll make sure you receive that tomorrow." And with that he hung up the phone.

I put the receiver down and shook my head.

~~~

The next day, after all the students were settled in class, Janet came into my office with a big smile on her face, holding up what looked like a bright pink purse. It was about six inches square, made of shiny material, and had a bright gold chain handle. Janet placed it down on my desk so that the front of the purse was facing me. In bright gold painted letters on the outside of the "purse" were the words *"Tiffany's Boo Boo Kit."*

"What's this?"

"Mrs. Allen dropped it off this morning for us to keep in the office."

Janet couldn't keep a straight face as she opened the purse for me to see. The inside included Dora the Explorer Band-Aids, a big tube of Neosporin, antiseptic pads, rubber gloves, and a note from Tiffany's parents. The note gave permission for the school to administer the contents of the *Boo Boo Kit* to Tiffany if she ever needed first aid at school in the future.

The kit was carefully housed on a shelf among the EpiPens, seizure medications and insulin shots.

I chuckled as I looked at Janet. "Well, this is a first for me. Have you ever seen a *Boo Boo Kit* at school before?"

Why Didn't He Tell Us?

I looked up when I heard their voices. Debra, the yard duty supervisor, was headed down the hall to my office and Eddie was right behind her with a scowl on his face. "You sit here and wait for the principal," she huffed.

He plopped down on the bench outside my office and folded his arms across his chest with a snort. "This school is not good for kids, this is not a good school," he snarled, as he furrowed his brow and pursed his lips.

I motioned Debra into my office and shut the door.

She raised her eyebrows, rolled her eyes and began to disclose the story. "This happened at the end of recess. Kenny and Colin were playing when Eddie came up and shoved Kenny into a tree. Kenny hit his head pretty hard. I don't know why Eddie did it. Colin ran over to me to tell me what happened. I motioned for Eddie to come over to me but he just ran away. I found him where his class was lining up. He was trying to hide behind some of the kids in line. As I approached him he did come out and I told him he needed to come to the office with me."

"Where is Kenny right now?"

"He's getting some ice on his head. He'll be OK but he was shaken up."

She went on to explain that Kenny told her he was playing a game with Colin when Eddie came over for no reason and shoved him. He lost his balance and fell into the tree. I don't know what's wrong with Eddie. This happens so often. He's such an angry little boy."

I thanked her and leaned back in my chair with a sigh. It had been no more than three hours since I'd played a game with Eddie because of his good behavior. It was a new game I'd never played before and he had been thrilled to teach it to me. This was so disappointing! Just when I thought we were making good progress, he exploded. The odd thing about this situation was that it didn't seem to have a trigger. Usually there was something that precipitated the outburst. I decided to let Eddie cool down a bit before talking with him. Best to allow that first burst of anger to dissipate, making it easier to get to the root of what happened.

I went into the office to find Kenny and see if he could talk. He was sitting in the "sick bay" with an ice pack on his forehead and when I walked in he looked up at me as if he was about to cry. I was pleased to, at least, see no blood, huge bumps or scrapes on his body.

"Kenny, do you feel like talking? I'd like to hear from you what happened on the yard."

He nodded and came into the office with me. He sat down in the chair, his feet dangling above the floor, holding the ice pack to his forehead.

"Show me where you hurt." He lifted the ice pack and pointed to a small red mark on his forehead. "So, tell me what happened."

He told me the same story that Debra had related. He added that when Eddie first pushed him he only lost his balance, and then Eddie pushed him a second time and that's what made him fall into the tree. He had no idea why Eddie did that; he hadn't even been playing with them. We talked a little more and I walked him back to the "sick bay" with his ice pack.

Now it was time to talk with Eddie. When I walked up to him he snapped. "This is a terrible place for kids to go to school. It doesn't help them at all."

"Let's go talk about it," I said and he followed me into my office. "I want to hear your side of what happened on the yard."

"I pushed Kenny and he fell into a tree. Then I ran away and hid and she found me and brought me here." He started crying. "I want my Mom, I want to go home, and I don't want to be here."

"Why did you push him?"

"I don't know"

"You don't know? You just pushed him?"

"Yes, he never plays with me. I want my Mom, can I go home now?"

We discussed why that wouldn't be happening right now. I decided to let him cool off a little more while I talked with Colin.

"You sit on the bench for a little. I'll be right back."

I went to Colin's classroom to talk with him outside. "Colin, I understand there was a problem on the yard at lunch recess."

"You mean when Eddie pushed Kenny?"

"Yes.

"Eddie was just protecting me"

"Really?" I felt surprised and relieved. "Tell me what happened?"

"We were playing and Kenny pushed me and was holding me down on the ground. He wouldn't let me up; he had his arm across my chest to pin me there. I was yelling at him to let me go. Eddie heard us and came over and pushed Kenny off of me and Kenny fell backward into the tree."

"Did you tell Debra that Eddie was protecting you when he pushed Kenny?"

"No, I just ran to get her when Kenny fell into the tree."

"Thank you Colin, I appreciate you telling me exactly what happened. You can go back in your class now."

That explained everything. I knew there had to be a reason I wasn't hearing. Eddie had outbursts that sent him from one to ten in two seconds, but there was usually a reason for them, and now I knew what this one was.

On my way back to the office Janet met me at the door. "Kenny's mother is here to pick him up. She's upset and wants to talk with you."

I walked back to the office to find Kenny and his mother waiting for me. I told her I had spoken with all the students involved in the situation and had some new information to share.

I looked at Kenny and said, "I just finished talking with Colin." Looking at Kenny's mother, I said, "Colin is the boy who was playing with Kenny when this incident happened." Then I continued. "Colin told me that you were holding him down on the ground and wouldn't let him go and Eddie came and pushed you to get you off of Colin." Kenny's eyes became very large and watery; he stared at me.

"Is that true, Kenny?" his Mother asked.

"Yes," said Kenny looking down at his feet.

I left Mother and son as she was questioning him about what really happened.

Back in my office I spoke with Eddie one more time

"Is it true that you pushed Kenny to get him off of Colin?"

"Yes, he wouldn't let him go; he kept holding him on the ground."

"Why didn't you tell Debra why you did it, or why didn't you tell me when I talked to you earlier?"

"I don't know, she was mad at me and I just wanted to get away from her, I didn't think she would believe me."

We talked some more and I praised Eddie for wanting to help his friend. We discussed different, more appropriate ways he could have handled the situation, and what he should do in the future. By that time Eddie was focused on other things.

"Do you know that I could have won the Walk-a-thon this morning?" he said.

That was the perplexing thing about Eddie. One minute you wanted to wring his neck and the next he could capture your heart with his seven-year-old grin.

 "What every child wants to know is, Do your eyes

light up when I enter the room? Did you hear me and did what I say mean anything to you?" ~*Toni Morrison*

THE EIGHTH INNING

SOME PEOPLE SURPRISE YOU!

Unpredictable

*J*une was unpredictable! One minute she could be your best advocate, touting all the wonderful things you had done educating her children. And the next minute the school did nothing right, and you were ruining her child's life forever. That's how she was—either in full drive or reverse, never in park.

She was a large, buxom woman with a magnetic personality—her voice echoed throughout the hallways, letting everyone know when she was on campus. The biggest determiner of which June you saw at any given moment was what she had chosen to ingest that day. June was a drug addict; when she was on something, it was in your best interests to steer clear.

I really liked the sober June. She had a wicked sense of humor and had no problem laughing at herself. I remember one day in particular, sitting in a Student Success Team meeting together. We were discussing her first-grade daughter, Treana, who had difficulty controlling herself in the classroom and was prone to bursts of temper when something frustrated her. We tried everything we could to help Treana control her emotions. We didn't want her sent out of the classroom and missing instruction.

During the meeting June reached across the table exposing a large fresh scar across the inside of her wrist. She caught me glancing at it.

"You're probably wondering where I got that beauty, right?"

"Actually, yes, I was."

"Well, a few weeks ago I got into an argument with Treana's dad. He made me so mad that I swung at him. He ducked and my hand went right through our plate glass window." With that she let out a hearty laugh and said, "Does that give you a clue about Treana's temper? Guess she must have learned it from me."

That's exactly what I was thinking. I was convinced June tried to be a good mother to her children. She had four of them, from three different fathers: a daughter in middle school, a daughter in fifth grade, a son in second grade and Treana in first. I tried to imagine what life was like in June's house. With the yelling and swearing I had heard at school it was pretty clear how inconsistent the parenting was for her kids and then, to top it off, when she was high on something she could be downright mean and angry.

~~~

I remember one particular day seeing the angry side of June. It was the day after we had called Child Protective Services (CPS) because of something one of her kids reported. She came storming down to the school, entered the lobby and started yelling.

"Where the f--- is the principal? I'm sick and tired of you guys meddling in my personal life. I want to know why the f--- you called CPS?"

I heard the commotion outside my office as Janet, our office manager, popped into my room.

"Do you hear that?" she asked.

"Yes, be ready to call the police if we need to. I'm not sure I can calm her down and I'm not sure she won't hit me. Get Pam and Andrea and have them come here right now."

Pam, our counselor, and Andrea, our school psychologist both knew June quite well and had good relationships with her, as did I, unless she was like this. I sure didn't want to be having this conversation with her by myself.

I tried to keep a little distance as I approached June and began talking. She was huge and strong and, to be honest, I was fearful of her at this moment. My heart raced. This was one of those times where I wished I could slip out the back door of the principal's office.

Luckily she had her aunt with her, who was good at calming her down. Her aunt tried to take her arm and steer her away, but June threw the woman's' hand off as she saw me.

"Why did you guys call CPS? What the hell are you trying to do? Have my kids taken away from me? You have no f---ing business doing that."

"CPS was here yesterday to see Omari but they never tell us who called them so we don't always know."

"I know it was you guys," she yelled stepping toward me.

I took a step backwards and tensed up.

"You're always butting your f---ing noses in where they don't belong."

With that her aunt grabbed her arm and said, "June, we need to leave now. Come on, this is not okay."

June thrashed her arm free, but she did stop. "You haven't seen the last of me yet," she yelled at me. Then she turned and stormed out of the school spouting profanities all the way out the door with her aunt by her side

I could see Andrea and Pam rushing down the hall as June was leaving. They looked at me and quickly ushered me inside my office. I must have looked like I was about to faint. I sat down in my desk chair and took a few deep breaths to calm down.

"You know, it scares me to think of what she could have done, or what I might have done if she had laid a hand on me."

~~~

247

The next day, June came by the office and asked to speak to me. This was the other June I knew, the one I liked, who might or might not remember the encounter we had the day before.

"My aunt told me what happened yesterday, and I apologize for my behavior. I know you have to do what you have to do. I'm trying really hard to be a good mom. My biggest fear is that they will take my children away from me."

In all of my years as an administrator I've never met a parent who didn't want the best education for his/her child. I have however met a few like June, who didn't always know the most effective methods to use in supporting their child's educational success.

 "Children learn more from what you are than what you teach." ~W. E. B. DuBois

The Lockdown

*I*t was a beautiful sunny day on the playground. The kids were out for recess playing tetherball and dodgeball and generally loving being outside and letting off steam. I was enjoying being out of my office, soaking up the sunshine while watching, and talking to the students when I received a phone call from another principal in the district.

"Jane, did you hear about the lockdown at the high school?"

"What? No I didn't, thanks. I'd better go check with my office."

I got off my phone and raced inside. My mind whirled with questions. *What does this mean for our school? The high school was only two blocks away!* As I approached, Janet, our office manager was rushing out to tell me what had happened.

"The high school is on lockdown! The police were chasing a car two guys had stolen. They drove off the freeway, crashed into a gate in front of the school, and ran away on foot. No one knows where they are. Should we go on lockdown too?"

I tried to process the information and make decisions quickly about what to do first, next and next. *Yes, of course we need to get all students into their classrooms. We're just down the street and we don't know which direction the suspects have run. It's recess so we follow our emergency procedures for a lockdown. We have to get word to those on yard duty to have the kids go straight to their classrooms. We also need to get the rest of the staff to return to their classrooms, and this all has to be done on the PA system without causing a panic.*

"Yes we do need to lockdown. Don't say too much on the PA. We don't want to scare the kids. Just tell the teachers to get back to their classrooms, lock their doors and close their blinds."

Parents were starting to call and ask what was happening. Some saw the rash of police action and helicopters, and heard sirens. They were getting reports on social media and were frantic to know what was going on.

"Tell the parents we're fine, we're on lockdown because of something at the high school, their kids are safe and we need to get off the phone. Call the district office and make sure the superintendent knows about the situation. Also, email all the staff and give them a brief update. They know to check their email. If we have substitutes in classrooms call them on their cell phones because they won't receive the email. Leave school phone lines open as much as possible for emergency updates from police and/or the district office."

Right then our psychologist walked into the office and I quickly set us both into action. "Andrea, you check the field side and I'll start checking from the street side. Make sure there are no students in bathrooms or out of their classrooms. Verify that all classroom doors are locked and blinds are closed. We'll reconvene back here."

As I walked out to the yard I looked around. It was eerie walking on campus with no other person in sight. It felt like a Sunday afternoon. But at the same time I had this vulnerable feeling; *if there was an intruder I was right out in the open.* But no time to think about that, I was in charge and it was my job to make sure the students were safe.

It took us about fifteen minutes to ensure the campus was secure. I went back to the office. Were there any updates?

We learned that the police had apprehended one of the suspects on the high school grounds, but that the other one had fled on foot down the street and away from our school. We needed to stay on lockdown though, until the police gave us the all clear to go back to normal business.

Go back to "normal business?" What would that look like with a school full of students, whose mental state ranged from not having a clue about the situation (mostly kindergarteners and first graders whose teachers told them we were having a practice drill), to many older students who were frightened, anxious and in some cases crying?

After about 45 minutes a police officer arrived. He had been sent to see that we were following procedures and were safe. I told him we had just checked to make sure all classrooms were locked and no students were outside. He wanted to see for himself so he and Ben, our new custodian, and I walked the campus again, checking inside all bathrooms and storage areas. As we were standing outside a fourth grade classroom a female student walked out of the door.

"Where are you going?" I asked

"To the bathroom."

"Not by yourself."

Before I could say anything else she hustled back inside her room. I was astounded the teacher would let her leave the classroom during a shelter-in-place lockdown, and by herself! Surprisingly the policeman didn't say anything. There would be a later conversation with the teacher.

We continued our safety check, and when the officer was satisfied that we were sheltered in place, he notified his police chief and was told it was safe for us to lift the lockdown. He was very kind and thanked us for doing such an organized and efficient job securing our campus. He assured us he would stay in our parking lot until the second suspect was captured, just as a precautionary measure.

We announced on the PA system that teachers could now unlock their doors and open their blinds. I sensed a feeling of relief in our office. We had done it! We had secured the campus! Most everyone had done their jobs well. Our staff could be very proud of how they had handled the situation. An email blast was sent out to parents letting them know the shelter-in-place lockdown was over and we were resuming normal school activities.

I figured we would have some very nervous and frightened students, so I went around to all the classrooms starting with fifth grade. They had been hearing a lot of speculation and misinformation as some were getting texts from their parents because they had siblings at the high school.

"I wanted to let you know exactly what happened this morning that caused our school to lockdown." I gave the students a brief update of what had happened.

"Were they murderers," asked a wide-eyed fifth grade girl.

"No, not at all," I assured them. It was two people who had stolen a car and the police have the two suspects in custody at the police station."

"I remember when someone stole a car in my neighborhood. Did they have guns or knives," asked Peter.

"No, Peter, there were no guns or knives involved."

There was one more question about if any clowns were involved? (There had been national media reports of creepy clown sightings that many students knew about.) I spent about fifteen minutes in each fifth grade class. Many students had stories they wanted to share about situations they had experienced. It was good for them to talk through the incident.

By the time I reached kindergarten, first and second grade, where most of the teachers had told their classes we were having a practice drill, everyone was settled, calm and engaged in their normal day.

I returned to my office relieved all had gone so well. As I was sitting there, the police chief came in. He wanted to personally tell me what had happened and to check in and make sure we were doing okay.

"Thank you for going on lockdown at your school and being so cooperative with us," he told me. "We didn't know at first which direction the suspect on foot had fled so we wanted to make sure all the kids were safe."

"Well, as nerve wracking as it was it was good practice for us. We've never had to do an official lockdown before so it's good to know our systems we put in place will work."

"I'm going to relieve the officer that has been stationed in your parking lot. Now that we have both suspects in custody you won't need him there any more."

We spoke for a bit about emergency situations, and then he left.

Janet came in and sat down. We looked at each other and sighed.

"You did a magnificent job," I told her. "For someone who has never gone through this before, you handled it beautifully. Thank you for being so calm and thoughtful."

We agreed that in a lockdown like this there's no time to stop and reflect until things are settled. You just do what needs to be done, which is why schools have emergency plans in place and practice them regularly. We need to review the processes for different kinds of emergencies because, even though they're written down on paper, luckily we're not given many opportunities to practice.

After lunch we sent an email to staff asking for their feedback, so we could learn from the situation. One thing we did learn is that we really need to have a contingency plan in place for when nature calls during a lockdown.

 "Courage is not the absence of fear, but the capacity to act despite our fears." *~John McCain*

Maybe It's Time to Retire

I really didn't know exactly how I should handle the situation with Martha Sampson. Martha had been teaching for about forty years and thirty-eight of those years were before I became principal of Baxter Elementary. In the short time I knew her I had grown very fond of her. She was about five feet tall with frizzy-reddish hair, bright blue eyes and a wicked sense of humor. Martha was amused with just about every situation that happened at school and always was ready with a quip she'd slyly mention to me.

But Darius was not one of those humorous situations Martha took delight in, and as I glanced out my office door I could see him sitting in one of the leather chairs facing Janet, our Office Manager. That meant he was probably waiting to see me again. His feet couldn't touch the floor so he was swinging them back and forth, his chin was drooped down on his chest and his shoulders were slumped over so I could only see the top of his head.

Janet walked into my office. "Martha sent Darius down again, apparently he was blurting out in class and disrupting others."

"Did she give you any details about what 'blurting out' meant? What exactly did he do?"

"Nope, she didn't. She just said that she'd had it with him."

That scenario happened at least weekly. It seemed that Darius spent as much time in the office as he did in his classroom. I walked into the office lobby and looked at him. He stopped swinging his feet and looked up at me with his big puppy dog eyes.

"I didn't do anything. She sent me down here for nothing. She just doesn't like me."

"Come on in Darius and let's talk. I want to know what you were doing when Mrs. Sampson sent you down here."

We talked for a while and what I heard was a repeat story of the time before and the time before that. Darius was asked to do something and he didn't do it, Mrs. Sampson raised her voice at him, and he responded by yelling back, "I don't want to do that," and refusing to do what she asked, so she sent him to the office for disruption and defiance.

I was tempted to call Pam, our Intervention Specialist, again, as I had done many times before, but stopped myself. That was exactly what he wanted. He really liked Pam and I sensed that he might be using these incidents as opportunities to get to talk with her and maybe play a game. So, I talked with him myself, calmed him down and eventually walked him back to his classroom.

However, dealing with Darius was the lesser of the problems here. The greater concern was Martha and her classroom management. How was I going to resolve that situation?

After school was out for the day I walked down to Martha's classroom. She looked up at me as I entered the room.

"Do you have a minute to talk about the Darius situation today?"

"Sure. That kid is driving me nuts. He's always blurting out in class, interrupting me and stopping others from learning. I needed to have him out of the classroom."

"I understand that, Martha, but this is happening weekly. And this same situation happened in the fall with Leroy and last year with Alonso and Le Shawn. Remember how frustrated you became with them? What can I do to help you deal with these little boys? It appears that whatever strategies you're using aren't working well and they can't just continue being sent to the office."

"I don't know. Maybe I just need to have Pam come sit with him in the classroom and redirect him when he gets out of sorts."

"Unfortunately I think that's exactly what he wants to have happen. He loves spending time with Pam. What if we used her as a reward for positive behavior?"

We talked for a while about how that would work.

"Pam's good at creating positive behavior charts for students." I mentioned. I'm sure she could help you create one for Darius."

"That might work."

"We could also provide a sub for you to go visit some other first grade teachers here or at another school. You could see what classroom management strategies they use."

"Yeah, I guess I could do that." Martha replied.

"What about a workshop or conference on classroom management? We have some funds available to pay for one."

"I'll think about that. Thank you."

After that conversation, things settled down for Darius and Martha. We developed a plan where he could spend time with Pam after a certain amount of time on good behavior; Martha observed other first grade teachers at our school, and we didn't see Darius in the office for a couple of months.

That March, Martha turned in her letter of resignation. She told me she had been thinking about it for a while, and since her husband was retired they could now spend more time traveling together. We shared a big hug and I told her I thought she was making the right decision.

Two years later I was at a retirement party for another teacher and Martha was there. She came up to me and said, "Thanks so much for nudging me out the door. Retiring was the best decision I ever made." I guess I wasn't as subtle as I thought I had been."

Surprise From Behind

*S*haron felt a sharp impact on the back of her head. Pain caused her to collapse to her knees and out of the corner of her eye she saw something fall to the ground. Glancing behind her she saw Martin standing, staring at her wide-eyed.

Martin was a tall, lanky 10-year-old boy with curly blonde hair and piercing brown eyes. Since his arrival at Baxter two months before, things had not gone right for him, or for anyone else in his classroom. Today, Martin was upset because his mother had brought him to school late after a morning doctor's appointment. When he was out of sorts it affected all the students and teachers around him.

Martin was enrolled in our district Counseling Enriched Class (CEC). Sharon was his teacher, very experienced in teaching general ed and special ed classes, but new to teaching the CEC. There were six third and fifth grade students in the class this year and Sharon enjoyed working with this population, taking great pride in providing individualized instruction and behavior modification. She had been working very closely with Martin, his parents, and the school psychologist, trying to get his behavior under control. But today Martin was not listening to anybody. He refused to do his work, wouldn't go to the time out room and was yelling at the teachers.

"You can't make me do anything. You're all stupid, and you don't know what you're doing."

Sharon and Debra, her Special Services Aide, had worked with him all morning, but he stubbornly would do nothing they asked. Sharon had just given him an assignment and had turned around to walk to her desk when she felt the impact on her head.

"Oh my god, Sharon, are you okay?" Debra quickly knelt by her side.

"I don't know, what just happened?" she responded, rubbing the back of her head.

"Martin threw a book at you."

"What?" She turned to look at Martin.

Reacting quickly, Debra instructed a classroom aide to take the class and hustled Sharon to the office. Janet called home for someone to come to school immediately and remove Martin. We sent Andrea, our school psychologist into the classroom to be with him until his family arrived, and then remain with the rest of the students.

Mom arrived quickly, rushing into the classroom. She was accustomed to this and it was always in the back of her mind that she might receive this phone call.

"I'm so sorry. Where is he?"

"In the time-out room with Andrea."

She ran to Martin and immediately withdrew him from school. It wasn't necessary to talk to anyone right now, she would do that later.

With the classroom settled, we could focus on support for Sharon. We put an ice pack on her head and called Gary, a nurse hired by the district to support severely disabled students in another class. He checked Sharon to see if we needed to call 911 or just take her to her doctor and It was determined that a doctor should see her. Together she and I drove to the medical center.

Sharon was injured physically, that was obvious, but what she reacted to more was the emotional impact of having a student, whom she thought she had developed a good relationship with, throw a book at her. She was distraught and shaking as I sat next to her in the car. Her eyes brimmed with tears.

"I know he didn't mean to hurt me. I'm just so surprised he did that."

" Yeah, I know. How badly does your head hurt?"

"It's sore. I'm starting to get a migraine."

She began telling me about her class and the history of why each of the six students was placed in the CEC. It was obvious she cared deeply about them because, although she was in pain, she wanted me to understand each of their stories, particularly Martin's. She was convinced he needed a smaller therapeutic learning environment to help him understand and overcome his negative behaviors.

Sharon was animated and I listened as she talked. Her conversation must have been a subconscious mental distraction to keep from thinking what she didn't want to think. I was surprised she didn't show anger toward Martin.

As it turned out Sharon suffered a concussion and was out of school for more than a week. When she returned to work she came into my office that morning. We had talked on the phone but this was the first time I had seen her since the accident.

"You look good," I said to her, hesitatingly. "Are you really okay? I mean mentally as well as physically."

"I'm fine," she replied. "The doctor gave me the clearance to return to work even though I am still experiencing some headaches but they're much less severe than I was feeling. He said that's normal"

"Are you sure?" I asked her. "I don't want you to be here if you're not up to it. Being with kids all day is not without stress. I'm fine with you staying home longer if you need to."

"No, I'm good. I'm actually anxious to get back to my class. I'll be fine."

"Okay, but please let us know if there's anything you need or if your headaches get worse and you need to leave." I assured her. "We did let you know that Martin will not be returning to the district. We met with the support staff and were able to find a non- public school placement that should work well for him."

"Yes, you did let me know that, I really appreciate your support in this situation, I just feel bad for him." replied Sharon and she left for her classroom.

Martin was suspended and was home schooled for a couple of weeks until the alternative placement was available where additional specialized supports not available in our CEC would be put in place to help him succeed.

 "Forgiveness says you are given another chance to make a new beginning." *~Desmond Tutu*

Dress Code for Parents?

It was Back to School Night and the Parent's Club president had started her presentation. I noticed the woman as she walked into the cafeteria late. She was of medium height, slim, and had short, blond disheveled hair with about an inch of dark brown roots. She was wearing a full-length light-pink, clingy, maxi dress, and was an attractive woman by most standards. At closer look, I could see that her hair was arranged unusually, with several small pony tails banded individually on all sides of her head. It looked as if she had been in the middle of letting her young daughter style it when she realized she was going to be late for Back to School Night, so quickly grabbed her purse and headed out the door, forgetting about her hairdo.

Aside from her looks, what also caught my attention was that when she came in late. Instead of just sitting in one of the chairs by the door, she entered one of the rows occupied by other parents and wiggled down it, saying "excuse me" several times, until she came to an empty seat where she sat down. She elicited many raised eyebrows and sideways looks as she passed through the row to her seat.

Immediately she began talking to the woman next to her. Several around her had to turn and quietly whisper "sssh" so they could hear the speaker. She would oblige and then after a few seconds turn back to her neighbor and continue her conversation. This went on throughout most of the presentation. It appeared that the woman was not concerned with what the speaker had to say or the wishes of those around her, but only with what was important to her.

When the speaker finished, everyone stood up and applauded. As the late-arriving woman stood up and bent down to pick up her purse, it was apparent to all who could see that she was wearing black thong underwear underneath her light-pink dress. *Ooops*, I thought. My grandmother had a saying she would have used in this situation, *I don't think she looked in the mirror from behind before she walked out the door.*

I don't like to pass judgment on people before I know them, but I formed some pretty significant conclusions about this woman. My mother used to say a person forms an opinion about you in the first 15 seconds. I always thought it was an unfair notion when thinking about someone meeting me for the first time, but here I was passing judgment in the same way on someone who was most likely very nice. I felt a little guilty. I figured she had to be the mother of one of our students, so I made a promise to myself to find out who she was and get to know her. Maybe I would turn around some of my pre-conceived ideas. But not tonight! She was immediately off and out the door, probably on her way to her child's classroom, and I was on my way to do my annual Back to School Night classroom visitations.

~~~

At the end of the evening I was talking with Paula, a first grade teacher and as we discussed Farley, one of her students, she told me what a difficult time he was having coming to school each day.

"His mother brings him to school and waits in line with him every day. He seems okay in line, but as soon as I come out to take the kids into class he suddenly has a stomachache or a headache and convinces Mom he feels too sick to stay. So she leaves and takes him home."

"Has this been going on since school started?"

"Yep, for about five days now. One day we did get him into the classroom, and she agreed to leave. But when she left she made such a huge production out of saying goodbye and then knocking on the window and waving to him as she walked outside, that it upset him more. He did finally calm down and the rest of the day he was happy and playing with his friends."

"Have you talked with her about just saying goodbye as he lines up, and then leaving?"

"Yes, I told her what works best is the parent drops their child off, tells them to have a great day, gives a kiss, and goes. I told her this happens regularly at the beginning of the year in kindergarten where kids are sad to leave their parents, but rarely in first grade. I think it's Mom who has the separation anxiety, and she is passing it along to Farley. I just don't know what else to do. Would you mind calling her for me?"

"Sure, no problem. I'll give her a call tomorrow."

"Just a side bit of information." Paula pointed out. "There was something odd about her tonight. She seemed a little out of touch with things, and I don't know if you saw her but she had the weirdest hairdo ever. She had these little ponytails coming out of all sides of her head. It looked like her four year old daughter had done her hair for her."

"I know just who you're talking about."

Perhaps this would be my opportunity to seize the moment and hopefully correct some judgments I'd made based on a fifteen second observation. I would call Farley's mom in the morning and have her come in and talk with me about successfully leaving him at school. Maybe I would gain some insights that would help us with Farley.

~~~

As it turned out, we soon learned more about Farley's home situation. When I called to schedule an appointment it was Farley's dad who answered the phone. He understood our concerns and requested an appointment to meet with us tomorrow if possible, by himself.

In our conversation the next day with Dad, we discovered Mom had a substance abuse problem. She was dependent on Farley and that's why she had difficulty leaving him at school. This caused Farley's reluctance to leave his mother because he felt she needed him. She was unknowingly encouraging her son to become an enabler.

Wow, this was not going to be an easy solution but our job was to focus on getting Farley into school, so we scheduled a meeting for later that week and included our school psychologist. Hopefully she could help us support Farley in being comfortable leaving his mom and staying at school while also working with his family to support their son's education.

A Student is Missing!

*P*anic set in! It was that awful feeling in the pit of your stomach when you find one of your students missing.

Extended day kindergarten had just started that year, and this was the first week the kindergarteners were eating in the lunchroom rather than in their classrooms. After lunch they went out to spend recess in the big playground where all the other kids played.

Today was Wednesday, and the third day of this procedure. It had been going smoothly so far. We had a plethora of noon duty supervisors on hand to help with lunchroom needs.

"How do I open this soy sauce?"

"I can't get the straw inside this box.'"

"How do you get the catsup out?"

"Oh, oh, my milk just spilled."

"I'm finished. What do I do now?"

As anticipated, there were many more needs from these kindergartners than from the older kids but we finally got all the numerous spills wiped up and encouraged just about everyone to eat something. We reminded ourselves to send a note home to parents, encouraging them to reduce the amount of food packed for these little guys.

"Everyone, gather what you haven't eaten and put it in your lunchbox, close it up and place it in your room's cart at the end of your table. Go back, sit down, and we'll excuse the table that's ready first."

Finally, everyone left the tables and eagerly headed out to the big yard. We were pretty impressed with ourselves. It was only the third day, and all the kindergartners were out on the play structure; no stragglers.

At the end of their recess we decided to make sure we got the younger kids off the equipment five minutes before the fourth and fifth-graders came out after their lunch. We didn't want any confusion and/or collisions. The older kids usually converged on the yard 'en-masse' and it could create an intimidating situation for the smaller kindergartners.

That process went smoothly. When the whistle blew all the kindergartners got down and ran to where their teachers were waiting for them to line up. I watched as all the teachers but one escorted their students back to class. Gina Winter's group was still waiting as I walked over.

"I only have 21 students. Cole is missing. Could he be in the bathroom?"

"You go ahead and take the rest of the kids inside. The yard duty staff and I will look for Cole."

We checked all the bathrooms, but no Cole. I asked the others to spread out and search every corner of the yard. By now we had over one hundred and fifty fourth and fifth graders covering all of the play area, which made it even more difficult to see one little guy. I went back to Gina's class to get a picture of Cole, so we all knew who we were looking for. We contacted the office to see if by chance a parent had come to dismiss him early and hadn't let the teacher know.

My heart started to beat a little faster now. Where could this kindergartner be? I checked all the other classrooms to see if perhaps he had gone into the wrong one. He wasn't in any of them. By now, word had spread and we had many adults looking for Cole.

My mind raced. Do I call the parents yet? Do we need to get the police involved? We don't want too much time to pass as we looked for him. Everywhere I went on campus there was another adult looking for Cole. We were scouring the school. Was the back fence around the playground locked? Ben, our new custodian made sure to do that every morning after students were in class. But we needed to check to make sure that he had done it today.

We were on our walkie talkies communicating with each other. Keep calm, I kept telling myself, he must be somewhere on campus. I walked out to the playground to check one more time for any word on Cole.

As I looked across the yard, I saw Andrea, our school psychologist. She was walking toward me with a little boy. It was Cole!

With a huge sigh of relief I rushed over to where they were. She had her arms around him and I could see that he was crying.

"Cole, I am so happy to see you!"

"I found him behind the dumpster. He didn't hear the whistle, so was still on the play structure when the big kids came out. He got frightened and ran and hid. He heard us calling for him but thought he was in trouble so he didn't come out."

Big tears streamed down Cole's face; I knelt down in front of him.

"Oh Cole, I am so sorry that happened. I can imagine how that must have felt with all those big kids running and climbing everywhere. That's scary . . . . Just so you know, they wouldn't have hurt you. They were only excited to have recess and get to play on the new curvy slide. So if that ever happens again, just know you're not in danger. They're your friends."

Whew, what a relief! Andrea escorted Cole back to class and I went to the office to send a message to all that our little lost kindergartner had been found. When I glanced up at my wall clock I had to look twice, surprised to discover that what had seemed like hours, had actually only lasted about 15 minutes!

Jumping to Conclusions

The day ended like any other day at school. The kids streamed out of their classrooms, some headed to the buses, some scattered in various directions out of school, and some met their parents to be driven home.

There was a bench in front of the school where some kids sat and waited for their rides. I was there saying goodbye to students when I noticed Tracey Chester patiently sitting on the bench looking for her mom's car. She and a couple of her friends chatted together and made comments at several of the boys passing by. The girls were in second grade and just beginning to notice the boys they thought were cute. Eddie was in Tracey's class and she had a crush on him. She thought that maybe he liked her too because sometimes she would catch him looking at her in class, and when he noticed she saw him he would look the other way. But many times he acted so weird around her like when he would come up behind her, tap her on the shoulder and then run away.

On this particular day, Tracey sat on the bench with her friends as Eddie and some other boys sauntered by. He tapped her on the shoulder and when she turned around he looked ahead and quickly walked away. He circled around again and as he went behind the

268

bench he stuck his fingers up through the bottom of the slats poking her in the bottom.

"Hey, what are you doing? Get away."

"I didn't do anything," he yelled as he ran away with his friends.

Right then Mrs. Chester arrived to pick up Tracy and her friends for a playdate. Tracey looked back as she and the girls piled into the car chatting animatedly as they buckled up their seatbelts.

"Did you see what Eddie did?" Tracy blurted out.

"No what?" asked Elise.

"He poked me in the butt."

"Eww, how gross. What did you do?"

" I just yelled at him to go away."

"What was that all about?" questioned Mrs. Chester from the front seat.

Tracey proceeded to tell her Mother about the incident that occurred on the bench.

Later that afternoon our office received a phone call from Walt Chester, Tracey's dad.

"I want to meet with Mrs. Blomstrand tomorrow about an incident that happened today with one of my daughters."

"May I tell Mrs. Blomstrand what occurred?" responded Janet.

"I'd rather discuss it with her tomorrow."

"Okay, she can meet with you at 8:00 tomorrow morning."

I always liked to have a heads up before meeting with a parent rather than go into a situation unprepared, so after school I caught up with Tracey's teacher to ask her if anything had happened with Tracey or her sister that would prompt Mr. Chester wanting to meet with me. She couldn't think of anything in particular. Both of the girls were doing well in school, and there were no discipline problems with either of them. Hmm, I thought, I guess I'll find out in the morning.

~~~

Bright and early before school started Mr. Chester arrived for our meeting. Janet called me on the phone in my office to tell me he was here, and I walked out to greet him. I was very curious to find out what this was all about. He was standing up when I entered. An attractive man, tall with broad shoulders and dressed nicely in a tan suit, blue button-down shirt and a paisley tie. His blond hair was trimmed in a very short crew cut. He stood with an air of confidence. I extended my hand.

"Hi, I'm Jane Blomstrand, nice to meet you. You must be Walt Chester, Tracey and Melissa's dad."

"Yes, I am, nice to meet you also."

"Come on down to my office where we can talk."

I motioned for him to sit down at the round table; he politely waited for me to sit before choosing a chair to occupy across from me.

"You have two lovely daughters, Mr. Chester. What can I help you with today?"

"I want to talk with you about a disturbing incident that happened after school yesterday involving my daughter Tracey and a boy in her class named Eddie."

He recounted what had happened yesterday while Tracey was sitting on the bench waiting for her ride home. His story involved Eddie repeatedly poking his daughter in the bottom, laughing with the other boys and not stopping when she nicely asked him to stop. I asked several questions and took careful notes on my letter-sized pad of paper. I would certainly investigate this incident. When he finished explaining the story that his daughter had told him he leaned forward on his forearms on the table, stared at me and said, "That is sexual harassment, Mrs. Blomstrand. What are you gonna do about it?" My initial thought after this posturing was that he was harassing me.

As his words registered with me, I internally took a deep breath before I responded. There would be no point in my taking the same tone with him as he took with me. I stood up, thanked him for bringing this to my attention and politely assured him that I would investigate the incident and get back to him later in the day. I told him my actions would be determined by what the investigation discovered.

After talking with Tracey, her teacher and the other students who were waiting in the same area where the incident happened, the truth unfolded. Eddie had poked her once through the slats in the bench, she told him to stop and he did. There was nothing to indicate sexual harassment had occurred. Eddie apologized to Tracey.

"I'm sorry Tracey, I didn't mean to hurt you."

"It's okay," Tracey quietly replied.

All the boys were spoken to about the importance of not touching other people's bodies and even if they did it to be funny it was not appropriate. I spoke to the parents of the boys to apprise them of the situation. Tracey's mother was notified of the results of the investigation, as I had been unable to reach her dad.

We never heard another word about the situation from Mr. Chester. It's a study in human nature how easy it is for some people to confront you when something is not right in their eyes. But, when the truth of the situation has surfaced many of those same people find it difficult to say "sorry" to have jumped to a hasty conclusion.

 "Stay open minded, things aren't always as they seem to be." *~Anonymous*

Feeling Safe

$\mathcal{I}$ was at a meeting with a colleague, Dina Vermont, another principal in Robinson USD, when her office manager called announcing that a student and mother wanted to talk with the principal. She invited them into her office. I actually knew the mother and her son, Jason.

"Is it okay if Mrs. Blomstrand is here?" asked Dina. "She's the principal at Baxter."

"Sure," said both the mom and the student.

They both sat down and I looked at Jason. "Hi Jason, it's good to see you."

He smiled a funny smile and looked at his mother.

"Its okay," she said. "You can tell them."

"I am transitioning," he declared. "I am no longer Jason, my new name is Joanie or J."

Mom said, "I call her J because it's easier."

"Thank you for telling me," said Dina. "I didn't know that. I appreciate you informing me in such a nice way."

A conversation ensued about how things were going for Joanie; about whether there had there been any bumps in the road and how communication went when she told others her news. The kids in the

272

classroom had been very accepting. Most of the adults had understood as well, but an uncomfortable situation had developed in music and that's why they wanted to talk with Ms. Vermont.

Evidently one day in music class, the students were playing their string instruments and the aide in the class asked a question of Joanie using her former name of Jason. Joanie politely told her the same thing she'd told us.

"I'm transitioning, I am no longer Jason, and my new name is Joanie or J. I would appreciate it if you would call me Joanie or J now.'"

Unfortunately the aide misinterpreted or didn't understand what she was saying and told her to go sit down and stop talking back and disrespecting her. Joanie wanted to share with Ms. Vermont that she didn't feel safe in the music class any more.

Dina listened carefully, leaning forward on the table towards Joanie. "I'm so sorry that happened Joanie. There are people at school who need more education on this issue because it's new for most of us. You have done such a wonderful job of educating your classmates I guess now it's time for me to help some of the adults understand as well."

She went on to tell Joanie that she was very proud of her and how she'd handled everything and how she was helping all of us learn what it's like to be transitioning, something most of us have had no experience with. Dina complimented Joanie on the wonderful job she was doing educating us.

Dina then asked if Joanie would like her to talk with the music aide before her strings class that afternoon.

Joanie responded quietly. "That would be very nice."

"Would you like me, as well, to come in while you are there to see how things are going? Or would you prefer that I be hands off and let you deal with it yourself?"

"I'm fine with either way."

Dina thanked Joanie for being so mature about dealing with others and their responses. "We are all learning from you Joanie," she repeated.

After Joanie and her mom left Dina and I commented on how much there still was to learn about students who were transitioning.

"Dina, I'm so impressed with how you handled that difficult conversation," I said. "This is new territory for most of us in education. We don't have manuals that guide us in dealing with students who are transitioning and you were very respectful to Joanie."

"Thanks, Joanie's parents came in to talk with me last week and explained that she had decided to make this transition. In that conversation they shared the challenges they had been through as a family helping her navigate this new territory. Joanie's mom said that once she knew she could look back and see signs since kindergarten."

"I can only imagine what it's like as a parent. There's so much we don't know about each other, sometimes even when you live in the same household."

Later that afternoon I saw Joanie on the playground playing basketball. I observed that she still wore the same clothes she did when she was Jason, loose basketball shorts, t-shirt, sweatshirt with hoodie and tennis shoes. Would she be switching to more female clothing? Maybe not yet; it didn't make any difference now. What was important was making Joanie feel comfortable and safe at school.

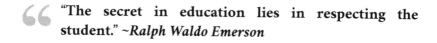

"The secret in education lies in respecting the student." ~*Ralph Waldo Emerson*

Our Reward

$\mathcal{T}$he staff and I celebrated when the letter arrived from The California Department of Education (CDE). We were thrilled! After four years of hard work our school had achieved substantial increases in student achievement. Baxter's Academic Performance Index (API) test scores had jumped 40 percent, almost 200 points. Now CDE was inviting us to present our story at the state's "On the Right Track Symposium."

The purpose of this symposium was for schools showing significant increases to share with other schools what they focused on at their site. It was a joint effort of the CDE and WestEd, a non-profit dedicated to improving education for all.

I read the letter at a staff meeting. The teachers stood up and cheered. We all shared a big round of applause. There were hugs, grins, and high fives throughout the room. Even a few tears of joy. We couldn't celebrate with champagne at school, so we toasted with sparkling cider.

"This means all your hard work is recognized outside our district. The many planning meetings together, implementing positive behavior management, training with coaches, and collaborating with each other, sharing best practices, paid off. It all worked and now is acknowledged by the state as effective. You guys should be proud of yourselves!"

We reflected back on the last four years.

"Remember when some of us went to visit Fred's school in Sacramento?" announced Ann. "We observed their class meetings and were so impressed and excited. I remember being nervous about bringing the idea back to our colleagues. Now everyone is holding class meetings."

"What about when we went to the trainings with the California Reading and Literacy Project (CRLP)?" exclaimed Paula. "We were jazzed about having their coaches come to our school but we didn't know how the rest of the staff would like strangers teaching in their classrooms. Now most of us look forward to the days when Karol and Marta are here."

"I think the frogs made the difference," Barry quipped. "The kids loved them."

Everybody laughed; Barry had been the one who suggested we give a tiny green beanbag frog to each student who was present for every day of testing. It had worked. We had almost perfect attendance.

Everyone agreed it wasn't always easy working together with the various personalities, methods of teaching, and levels of experience in our classrooms. But we made a pact to be respectful with each other and put in the effort to do what was thought to be effective for all students.

We reminisced about everything else that had happened at Baxter during those three years. The school had experienced its share of challenges.

"Think of all the obstacles we have been through since the state started the new testing program," lamented Ann, a third grade teacher. "Two years ago the district completely modernized our school. There was construction all around us, and classrooms rotated through portables on the yard. Remember that?"

"What about the tense negotiations between the school district and teacher's union, which ended in a strike?" retorted Ray, a fifth grade teacher. "We were out for a week."

"And we also had the awful attacks on the World Trade Center."

To the staff's credit those issues did not deter us from our goal. We had our ups and downs, but managed to work through those moments with grace.

"So what happens now?" Asked Ann. "How do we present at this symposium?"

"The state wants us to send a team of teachers and an administrator down to Southern California in April to make the presentation. We have to decide who'll be on that team to represent Baxter."

After lots of discussion, it was almost unanimous that Barry, Ray, Ann and Hannah would be the team. Hannah was our Literacy Specialist, and worked with students at all grade levels. Ann had been the lead on our Literacy Committee and was relentless in supporting the CRLP coaches. Barry had been one of the pioneers in implementing class meetings, and Ray had worked tirelessly with the fourth and fifth grade teachers.

Our work as a team began. The five of us rolled up our sleeves for weeks preparing the presentation. What would best give the message showing how we had accomplished such a big rise in test scores? Should we include some personal stories?

"Yes," suggested Barry. "Let's tell them about Naomi. When she started third grade she couldn't even read on a first-grade level. We had to do a home visit to get her mother to send her to school. Then when she started attending regularly she ended the year on grade level."

"I'll never forget how she beamed on stage when she got the perfect attendance award at the end of the year."

"What about Roberto?" Exclaimed Hannah. "He didn't know all his letters when he started first grade. He worked with one of our Reading Recovery teachers and was reading books by the end of the year."

"I remember watching him read "Go Dog Go" to one of our Project

Read volunteers. When he was finished he proudly asked, 'Do you want me to read it again?' "

Thinking about our students as we planned our presentation, we were reminded of what it all meant to them. Giving students the necessary foundation would help the Naomis and Robertos become, self-confident, productive citizens in our future society.

 "When the best leader's work is done the people say, "We did it ourselves." *~Lao-Tzu*

The Revolving Door of Superintendents

They came and went, each making their stamp on the Robinson Unified School District. In my six years as principal of Baxter Elementary there were five different men in the position of superintendent.

Don Stanton was superintendent when I began. Lots of drama swirled around him. The school board dismissed him the year before I arrived, sparking a contentious battle that ended in a recall of the three board members who ruled to oust him. He sued the district to get his job back and the new school board reinstated him the spring before I came on board. The district and community was split over his rehire. Of course I didn't know any of that drama when I accepted the job of principal.

Don was a big, quiet guy who carried a heavy stick. Luckily I started off on his good side and we got along well. He was also with me during the whole process when we delayed the start of school a week because of the asbestos found in classroom ceilings. If, however, you were on the wrong side of that invisible stick he carried, like the teachers' union leadership, you had a difficult time dealing with him. And so, in the second year of my job, we ended up with a difficult teacher's strike at the end of the year. Don didn't like the union leaders and they had no respect for him, so reaching a contract agreement was virtually impossible. They finally settled the contract 5 days before the end of the school year, but the school board ended up putting Don on administrative leave for the Fall, and he never returned to Robinson.

Because Don was on leave we ended up hiring an interim superintendent. Luckily for us Marshall Chandler recently retired as superintendent of a neighboring district, so he came on board to support us. Marshall was quiet like Don but he was the warm, caring grandfather type. He immediately visited every principal at our respective school sites and spent time getting to know us, learning our working relationship with staff and students. During Marshall's time Baxter had a complaint with ensuing newspaper coverage accusing a teacher in our Counseling Enriched Class (CEC) of putting kids in a "black box". It was mischaracterized in the newspaper. What the reporter called a "black box" was a "time-out" area for kids to go when they needed to let out their frustrations. We invited her to come visit the classroom and talk to the students, which she did, learning the truth of the matter, however, she never wrote an article for the newspaper about the reality of the class. Marshall was by my side the whole way as we resolved that awkward situation.

Of course since Marshall was officially retired, he had already planned a vacation during the winter months, so he left us in January and a second interim superintendent was selected. Bruce Gardner joined our district. He was more of a nondescript man and I don't remember much about him although I do remember one legacy he left our district. When he negotiated the union contract he agreed to increase our morning recess time from 15 to 20 minutes. Our prep schedule for teachers was created in 45-minute blocks, built around a 15-minute recess. Creating a new schedule before the year was over was a nightmare. He wasn't there for more than 5 months, but what a mess he left with that decision.

That summer the district hired a new superintendent, not an interim this time. It was my fourth year and Arthur Chen came on board. One month into his superintendency on September 11, 2001, the attacks on the Pentagon and World Trade Center occurred.

Those of us who were adults on that date will always remember where we were and what we were doing when the attacks happened. I was driving to work in my car when I heard the events unraveling on the radio. I pulled off to the side of the road to listen because I couldn't believe what I was hearing. After trying to process what happened my mind went immediately to how do we handle this when I get to school. We can't go through the day not saying anything, because that event will have affected every adult on campus dramatically, and some of our students most likely overheard their parents reacting to the news or worse yet watched the visuals on television.

We met as a staff before students arrived and agreed that each teacher would have a brief (appropriate-for-their-grade-level) conversation about the event in their classroom, and be prepared if they recognized a student having a difficult time dealing with the news. Our Intervention Specialist and Psychologist would be on site to talk with any troubled students.

Arthur skillfully guided us through that sorrow, but after one year he quit his job and left for another district. We were never sure why but our guess was the financial compensation. The district, reeling from another superintendent loss, decided to hire Wayne Russell. This was a decision they should have made two years earlier. Wayne had been the District Assistant Superintendent of Human Resources for many years and was the perfect person to lead our schools. He was personable, had a good relationship with the union leadership and the staff loved him. Wayne was a former PE teacher, and always wore his glasses perched on top of his head or way down on the end of his nose, he rolled his shirtsleeves up, and his tie loosened at his neck. He peered at you from above or below those glasses as he listened to your story. I enjoyed problem solving with Wayne.

Two situations occurred at Baxter on Wayne's watch. During his first year our school underwent a complete modernization process, moving in and out of classrooms all year. In his second year several teachers filed a sexual harassment suit against our head custodian. Both were very difficult situations to handle and I couldn't have asked for a better boss to lean on during that time. He taught me how important it is to be supported by those in charge. My only critique of Wayne was when the state invited us for a second year to present at the "On The Right Track" symposium he was unable to find the funds to send us. I felt sad that our team who worked so hard could not again share with other schools what they had learned.

~~~

Five different superintendents during my time as principal at Baxter didn't provide much consistency. They each were so busy learning the systems and the different people they needed to interact with that at the school sites we were pretty much left to make decisions on our own. For Baxter that was fine; we had implemented strategies and plans that were successful so we just continued doing what worked for our school and students. I was delighted when Wayne stayed and provided some stabilization for all of us so we could make plans together in the future.

 "You can't stop the waves but you can learn to surf." *~John Kabat-Zinn*

THE NINTH INNING

I WILL MISS ALL THAT!

The Reading First Giant

$\mathcal{T}$oday's meeting was for principals. The goal was to make sure we were on board with the district's new language arts program. Robinson USD had applied for the Federal Government's Reading First Grant, and had just learned the application was accepted. A new Coordinator of Language Arts, Shannon Brockman, was hired to oversee its implementation with full fidelity, a requirement of the grant. Shannon was running this meeting, along with two consultants from the state. All principals had to sign assurances of certain things we would implement at our school site.

~~~

Let me provide a little background of our school and language arts before continuing with what happened at the meeting

Reading and writing had been our focus for the past five years at Baxter. I mentioned that our school was invited to present at the state's "On the Right Track Symposium" because of the huge jump in our API score. One of the main reasons for our success was that a team of teachers, one from each grade level, and I had participated in five days of training with the California Reading and Literature Project

(CRLP). We learned effective research-based strategies for teaching reading and writing and shared them with the rest of the staff. All teachers worked closely with two coaches who came to Baxter four times a year and they provided demonstration lessons in classrooms. We provided substitutes allowing teachers to observe these lessons and then meet with the consultants to debrief. The coaches would also meet with and observe individual teachers upon request.

This was powerful professional development and was working, as demonstrated by the increase in the school's test scores. Our teachers were learning effective strategies and implementing them on a daily basis with students. We were proud of our school and the difference we were making in student achievement and learning.

When our district announced the new language arts program, some on our staff had concerns. One of them was Ann Roberts, a dynamic and excellent third grade teacher. She came to talk to me about the program.

"Jane," she lamented, "when I looked over the writing component of this program I saw some weak areas. I'd like to use what we learned with our coaches; it's so much stronger. Is it okay for me to supplement the writing part of this new program?"

"I totally understand your concern. You guys have worked hard to develop powerful strategies and they've proven effective. But the district has adopted this new program and they say it uses research-based strategies. It's important to test it out first. Otherwise you have little authority to say it doesn't work. Do that first and then you have my blessing to supplement with whatever you know has proven itself."

~~~

I reflected on that conversation as I sat in today's meeting and glanced down at Assurance #8: *Teachers will use only supplemental materials that are approved and aligned with the specified language arts program.*

Hmmm, I thought. What did that mean? Could Ann supplement

with the materials from the CRLP if she needed to? What supplemental materials were they referring to?

I leaned over to another principal who was also a former literacy specialist.

"Do you know what Assurance #8 means?"

"I don't, but I don't like it. Why don't you ask them?"

So, I asked the question. "Regarding Assurance #8, who decides what supplemental materials are approved? Is that the principal at the site? Is it the district office? Or is that a decision you make?"

"Why would your teachers need to supplement with any other materials? Everything is in the program and spelled out step-by-step, very easy for any teacher to follow."

"My teachers have had four years of professional development with the CRLP and have developed some very powerful research-based writing strategies that have proven effective. As they have begun to implement this new program, they have some concerns with the writing component. As they move forward they would like to infuse these strategies if needed."

The answer I received caused me to pause, and stare blankly at her.

"Everything they need to teach language arts is in this program spelled out step-by-step; they just need to look deeper and implement it correctly and it will work."

You've got to be kidding, I thought. I'm sure my frustration showed. My nine years of training as a literacy specialist before becoming a principal had taught me differently. One step-by-step approach can't teach all students. Any effective teacher always has to use the best strategies available to meet individual student needs. If that means supplementing with additional materials then that's what should be done.

Assurance #8 was a big issue for me. After all the excellent professional development my teachers had received, I was being asked to promise that they would implement a prescriptive program, step-by-step, without using the skills they had developed. I could see it would be a challenge to support my talented staff if I had to meet this

Assurance. However, since I was expecting them to give this new program a try, I felt I could sign the Assurances this year, but I could not promise to do so in the future.

---

66 "Education is not the learning of facts, but the training of the mind to think." *~Albert Einstein*

Final Word

$\mathcal{B}$eing a principal was the most rewarding job of my educational career. Leaving it for another position in the field was a difficult decision, but it was the right choice for me.

In the six years I was at Baxter my staff and I had worked together building a culture of support for students. We strengthened our language arts program, increasing student achievement. We created a school-wide positive behavior support system with common goals. We collaborated, recognizing the strengths each of us brought to the table. We provided support for our struggling students and those needing an extra challenge. We worked together with parents, creating high expectations for each student. We created a culture where teachers, students and parents felt safe, supported and respected, and we accomplished this one relationship at a time. All this had moved our school forward.

So when the district implemented the Reading First program I didn't want to lose all we had accomplished through our collaboration with the CRLP. But in fairness to the new program and the district, it was important to give it some time to settle in and see how it unfolded. Hopefully our experienced teachers would learn additional teaching strategies to add to their repertoire, and our new teachers would benefit from following a structured, proven approach to language arts instruction.

~~~

The next school year began and after several months of observing the implementation of the new Reading First Program, I knew in my heart that I was not the right person to lead this effort. The program placed more emphasis on seating arrangements, placement of phonics cards and which wall to locate specific bulletin boards than on effective teaching strategies. My staff had developed the "right stuff" to continue providing excellent education for students. It was just me! I couldn't ask the teachers to do something that I didn't believe in. The culture of support that had been created at Baxter would continue for our students without me. It was difficult; I loved the school, staff and students. I felt connected to them and would miss seeing the joy on the faces of students every day as they arrived at school. But, knowing I could not support the implementation of the Reading First Program I made the decision to leave for another position in education.

~~~

Two years later, in 2006, the U S Department of Education Inspector General's Office conducted a review of the Reading First Program's first 5 years and showed, among other things, that there was no data indicating an increase in reading comprehension among students being taught with the Reading First approved programs vs other research-based methods. That review reinforced my belief that, just as all third grade students don't wear the same size shoe, we shouldn't try to fit students into a language arts program that forces everyone onto the same page on the same day. We needed to respect the different educational needs of students.

~~~

As I reflect on all the stories in this book and my years as a principal, I am reminded of what is at the heart of education. It is the importance of positive and caring relationships and respect and how we must incorporate that daily into our academic environment. Students are in school for almost one third of their day, five days a week. That's a huge part of their lives, which means the kind of culture we provide can impact them in a major way.

I thought about Bernadette, one of our third graders. It was April before we found out that she and her parents had been living in their car and sometimes in a friend's garage. She always came to school on time, dressed nicely, and with homework in hand, but you can imagine what it took for her to get to school like that every day. Were we providing support for Bernadette and her parents?

Schools need to be much more than places for teaching curriculum. In today's society, schools have a greater responsibility. We need to serve as support systems for families like Bernadette's. We need to be places where students feel safe, know we support and care about them and where they can learn to show empathy for others and live respectfully in society.

What do we do to create that kind of culture for our students? How do we greet them when they daily arrive at school? That interaction can put a spark in a student's day or dampen a flame. When students have problems at school are they chastised or listened to and helped to see how they can change their behavior to achieve more positive results? Are students encouraged to take risks and allowed to learn from their mistakes, can they fail and learn from that experience? Does our staff believe in each student's ability to achieve success? Do we communicate with students to learn what their experience in school is like? We need to have systems in place that get to the heart of education and help our students mature into responsible members of our community.

I think about all these things when I coach new administrators. I listen to them share their experiences, unique challenges, and often-fleeting successes. I am constantly reminded of how much impact a leader has on a school and the people within that educational environment. A principal's primary mission is to create a culture that will move student achievement forward. To do that, he or she must carry the vision for the school, build positive relationships, and develop trust and respect among team members. That is accomplished through open dialogue and collaboration. Often we enter into a situation with a set idea that can change after hearing the other side. I try to encourage these new administrators to listen and learn from the people around them and value the strengths of each individual. At the end of the day teachers want to teach and students want to learn.

Just like baseball managers have a responsibility to the players, educators have a responsibility to students. Our daily interactions impact them in ways we may never realize, but down the road society may reap the rewards of our supportive culture or suffer the consequences of our ignorance and neglect.

 "In a completely rational society, the best of us would aspire to be teachers and the rest would have to settle for something else because passing civilization along from one generation to the next ought to be the highest honor and the biggest responsibility anyone could have." ~*Lee Iaccoca*

From the Author

Thanks for reading the book, I hope you enjoyed it. Please do let me know your thoughts and experiences. I would love to hear from you. You may reach me at Jane@MeetThePrincipal.com

May I ask you an important favor? If you enjoyed this book could you please take a moment and **leave me an honest REVIEW**. Just a line or two is enough to help me make this book visible on Amazon and other sites. The success of authors, such as myself, relies heavily upon reader reviews. Thank you.

~Jane Blomstrand

Acknowledgments

Through this process I came to realize that "it takes a village" to produce a book so I would like to offer my heartfelt appreciation to:

My writing teacher extraordinaire Nancy Henderson, who was persistent in trying to teach me to "show not tell."

My friend Diane Inman, for graciously meeting with me for two years, reading and editing each story, and letting me know what was missing and what questions were unanswered.

My friends Carolyn Reed and Toni McShane, for taking their time to edit these stories and give me honest feedback.

My friend and author Dan Hanel, for inspiring me to actually produce a book from my life as a principal.

My patient and honest editors, Jil Plummer for her encouragement, and William Gensburger for his incredible insight into the meaning of the stories.

My friend, Megan Majestic for her creativity in designing the connecting hands on the cover.

And last but not least to my husband Curt for red-lining my papers and providing the inspiration for me to continue, assuring me that there is someone out there other than my family who will want to read these stories.

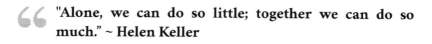"Alone, we can do so little; together we can do so much." ~ Helen Keller

Glossary

1. CDE California Department of Education:
An agency within the Government of California that oversees public education.

2. CEC Counseling Enriched Classroom:
A structured mental health program offering therapeutic interventions designed to help struggling students succeed in school.

3. CPS Child Protective Services:
A governmental agency responsible for providing child protection.

4. CRLP California Reading and Literature Project
A collaborative statewide network to provide high quality, standards-based teacher professional development in reading and academic language instruction.

5. EL English Learner
A person who is learning the English language in addition to his/her native language.

6. ELAC English Learner Advisory Committee

A committee comprised of parents, staff and community members specifically designated to advise school officials on English Learner program services.

7. ELD English Language Development

Instruction designed specifically to advance English Learners' knowledge and use of English in increasingly sophisticated ways.

8. GATE Gate and Talented Education

A broad term for special practices, procedures and theories used in the education of children who have been identified as gifted or talented academically.

9. Gen Ed General Education

The foundation of skills, knowledge, habits of mind and values that prepares students for success in their future.

10. IEP Individualized Education Plan

A document developed to meet individual educational goals for each public school student who qualifies for special education.

11. NPS Non Public School

Private non sectarian schools certified by the state of California to provide special education services to students.

12. OSHA Occupational Safety and Health Administration

A United States Department of Labor agency to assure safe and healthful working conditions for working men and women.

13. PC Parent's Club

An organization designed to support the education of students in partnership with a school.

14. PTA Parent and Teacher Association

A parent-teacher organization intended to facilitate parental participation in a school.

15. SARB School Attendance Review Board

An agency designed to provide a safety net for students with persistent attendance problems.

16. Special Ed Special Education

A program to provide students with disabilities which prevent them from fully benefitting from general education approaches with specialized instruction and intervention to enable them to benefit from their education.

17. SST Student Study Team

A group formed within the school usually consisting of a parent, teacher, administrator and/or support personnel to examine a student's academic, behavioral and social-emotional progress.

18. T K Transitional Kindergarten

A publicly funded program meant to be a bridge between pre-school and kindergarten for 4 year olds who will turn 5 between September 2nd and December 2nd.

19. WestEd *A non-profit organization working with education to promote excellence, achieve equity and improve learning for students.*

Made in the USA
San Bernardino, CA
11 November 2019

59722430R00173